FROM METAPHYSICS TO ETHICS

FROM METAPHYSICS TO ETHICS

A Defence of Conceptual Analysis

FRANK JACKSON

CLARENDON PRESS · OXFORD
1998

Oxford University Press, Great Clarendon Street, Oxford OX2 6DP
Oxford New York
Athens Auckland Bangkok Bogota Bombay
Buenos Aires Calcutta Cape Town Dar es Salaam
Delhi Florence Hong Kong Istanbul Karachi
Kuala Lumpur Madras Madrid Melbourne
Mexico City Nairobi Paris Singapore
Taipei Tokyo Toronto
and associated companies in
Berlin Ibadan

Oxford is a trade mark of Oxford University Press

Published in the United States by
Oxford University Press Inc., New York

British Library Cataloguing in Publication Data
Data available

Library of Congress Cataloging in Publication Data
Data available
ISBN 0-19-823618-2

1 3 5 7 9 10 8 6 4 2

Typeset by Invisible Ink
Printed in Great Britain
on acid-free paper by
Biddles Ltd, Guildford and King's Lynn

in memory of my father

PREFACE
AND ACKNOWLEDGEMENTS

I HAVE for many years championed the cause of conceptual analysis. When the very welcome invitation to give the John Locke lectures at Oxford arrived, I decided to use the occasion to articulate the important place I see for conceptual analysis in philosophical inquiry.

Conceptual analysis is currently out of favour, especially in North America. This is partly through misunderstanding its nature. Properly understood, conceptual analysis is not a mysterious activity discredited by Quine that seeks after the a priori in some hard-to-understand sense. It is, rather, something familiar to everyone, philosophers and non-philosophers alike—or so I argue. Another reason for its unpopularity is a failure to appreciate the need for conceptual analysis. The cost of repudiating it has not been sufficiently appreciated; without it, we cannot address a whole raft of important questions. And, as you might expect if I am right about our need for it, conceptual analysis is very widely practised—though not under the name of conceptual analysis. There is a lot of 'closet' conceptual analysis going on.

The book is concerned to put flesh on these roughly sketched bones. I see it as primarily addressed to sceptics about conceptual analysis, but I seek also to clarify matters for believers. Some practitioners of conceptual analysis at times give the impression that they are doing it in the spirit of, 'Well, I'm a *philosopher*, after all.' But, in fact, there is a perfectly straightforward 'external' justification for conceptual analysis. True, it's fun; true, it is what philosophers have traditionally spent a good deal of time doing; but the case for it can be grasped without initiation into the philosophical fellowship; there is, as we might put it, a folk case for it.

I have always been suspicious of excessively abstract theorizing in philosophy. I think that an important test of metaphilosophical claims is whether they make good sense in the context of particular problems. The discussion in the book is, accordingly, anchored in particular philosophical debates. The basic framework is

developed in the first three chapters via a consideration of the role
of conceptual analysis in the debate over the doctrine in metaphysics known as physicalism, with digressions on free will, meaning, personal identity, motion, and change, and then applied in the
last three chapters to current debates over colour and in ethics. As
a result, the book ends up being as much about physicalism,
colour, and ethics as about conceptual analysis.

I should say something about how the text that follows relates
to the lectures as delivered in the Trinity term of 1995. Each lecture
was an abbreviation of a considerably longer written text, and I
originally planned to publish these written texts more or less as
they stood; however, the many good objections, the many interesting further issues, and the many misunderstandings that arose at
the lectures (and elsewhere) convinced me that I should say considerably more. I have, however, retained the somewhat informal lecture tone and a certain amount of the recapping characteristic of
delivered lectures. What you have before you is, I suppose, the lectures as they would have been had they been delivered a year later
than they in fact were, and to an extraordinarily patient audience.

I am indebted to discussions at Oxford University, the Aus-
tralian National University, Cambridge University, Monash
University, and Simon Fraser University, and to comments from,
among those I remember, John Bigelow, David Braddon-Mitchell,
David Chalmers, Tim Crane, Chris Daly, Martin Davies, André
Gallois, Brian Garrett, Richard Holton, Lloyd Humberstone, Rae
Langton, Catherine Legg, Hugh Mellor, Peter Menzies, Adrian
Moore, Karen Neander, Daniel Nolan, Graham Oppy, Philip
Pettit, Jack Smart, Michael Smith, Barry Taylor, and, especially,
David Lewis. I have also expressed my indebtedness to particular
points at the relevant places in each chapter when it seemed appropriate and I could recall the source with confidence. I have a rather
different debt to Gilbert Harman and Michael Devitt. Their tren-
chant objections, both in their writings and discussion, convinced
me of the need to defend conceptual analysis.

In the first three chapters I draw on, very considerably expand,
and revise some things I say in 'Armchair Metaphysics', in John
O'Leary Hawthorne and Michaelis Michael, eds., *Philosophy in
Mind* (Dordrecht: Kluwer, 1994), 23–42 (with kind permission from
Kluwer Academic Publishers); 'Finding the Mind in the Natural

World', in Roberto Casati, Barry Smith, and Graham White, eds., *Philosophy and the Cognitive Sciences: Proceedings of the 16th International Wittgenstein Symposium* (Vienna: Hölder–Pichler–Tempsky, 1994), 101–12; 'Postscript', in Paul K. Moser and J. D. Trout, eds., *Contemporary Materialism* (London: Routledge, 1995), 184–9; and 'Metaphysics by Possible Cases', *Monist,* 77 (1994): 93–110. Chapter 4 is a revised and expanded version of 'The Primary Quality View of Color', in James Tomberlin, ed., *Philosophical Perspectives*, vol. x (Cambridge, Mass.: Basil Blackwell, 1996), 199–219, and appears with kind permission from the editor. The view of colour it puts forward is one I first heard from D. M. Armstrong (though he dissents from my unduly subjectivist, as he sees it, version), and came to accept after discussions with Robert Pargetter. We published a paper, 'An Objectivist's Guide to Subjectivism about Colour', *Revue International de Philosophie*, 41 (1987): 127–41, which contains an early version (and one in need of considerable revision and addition, I fear). Early versions of some of the ideas in Chapters 5 and 6 received a first, short outing in my critical notice of Susan Hurley, *Natural Reasons* (New York: Oxford University Press, 1989), *Australasian Journal of Philosophy*, 70 (1992): 475–88, and were further developed in Frank Jackson and Philip Pettit, 'Moral Functionalism and Moral Motivation', *Philosophical Quarterly*, 45 (1995): 20–40. These two papers prompted a lot of correspondence from doubters (and some from supporters), and these two chapters have been very significantly moulded by this correspondence. I also draw in Chapter 5 on the many discussions I had with Graham Oppy and Michael Smith about how to specify cognitivism in ethics during the writing of our paper 'Minimalism and Truth Aptness', *Mind*, 103 (1994): 287–302, but I decided to put the key point rather differently.

Finally, special thanks to Corpus Christi College, Oxford, for providing a wonderful environment.

Canberra   FCJ
February 1997

CONTENTS

CHAPTER I

Serious Metaphysics and Supervenience

WE will be concerned with the interconnections between three topics: metaphysics, supervenience, and conceptual analysis. In the first three chapters I present a general picture of how I see the relationship between our three topics. For concreteness and familiarity, I focus on the particular view in metaphysics variously known as (reductive) materialism or physicalism, and mostly address the issues within that framework; but the aim is to extract general morals. The upshot of our discussion will be a defence of the importance of conceptual analysis for metaphysics. This conclusion will be found shocking by many, but I hope to convince you, or more realistically some of you, that opposition to conceptual analysis is based on misunderstandings of what it is and a failure to appreciate its indispensability to metaphysics.

In the last three chapters I do some metaphysics. I discuss the metaphysics of colour and of ethical properties. As you would expect, given what I argue in the first three chapters, the appropriate conceptual analyses and supervenience theses play a central role in the discussion in these chapters. However, much of what I say here is relatively independent of what I say in the first three chapters—and when it isn't, I do a certain amount of 'saying again quickly'; in consequence, they are more or less free-standing.

In this first chapter I start by explaining how serious metaphysics by its very nature raises the location problem. I then argue that considerations arising from how supervenience theses elucidate completeness claims in metaphysics tell us that the location problem can only be solved by embracing what I call the 'entry by entailment' thesis. In the second chapter we make a start on how these matters connect with conceptual analysis.

SERIOUS METAPHYSICS AND THE LOCATION PROBLEM

First Example: Finding the Semantic Properties

Some physical structures are true. For example, if I were to utter a token of the type 'Grass is green', the structure I would thereby bring into existence would be true, and it would be true in part because of how things are and in part because of its meaning or content and the reference of its parts.[1] The object I would thereby bring into existence would also have a certain mass and length (or duration), a certain causal and evolutionary history, be of a type the other tokens of which have characteristic causes and effects in my mouth and from my pen, and in the mouths and from the pens of my language community, have a certain structure the parts of which have typical causes and effects, and so on. How are the semantic properties of the sentence related to the non-semantic properties of the sentence? Where, if anywhere, are the semantic properties of truth, content, and reference to be found in the non-semantic, physical or naturalistic account of the sentence?

We might respond with a sceptical or eliminativist position on truth, meaning and reference. Sentences are, when all is said and done, a species of physical object, and we know that science can in principle tell us the whole story about physical objects. And though we are not yet, and may never be, in a position actually to give that whole story, we know enough as of now to be able to say, first, that it will look something like the story I gave a glimpse of— a story about masses, shapes, causal chains, behavioural dispositions of language users, evolutionary history, and the like—and, secondly, that in any case it will not contain terms for truth, reference, and meaning. But if the complete account does not contain truth, reference, and meaning, then so much the worse for truth, reference, and meaning, runs the sceptical response.

Alternatively, we might respond by distinguishing what appears explicitly in an account from what appears implicitly in it. Suppose

---

[1] It would be true in English, and also true *simpliciter*, as I would be speaking English. Incidentally, the point being made does not depend on taking a view on whether sentences are more fundamental bearers of truth than are, say, beliefs or propositions—whatever precisely that issue comes to. What matters is that sentences—the marks on paper or sound-wave patterns—are true, have content, and have parts that refer.

I utter the sentence, 'Jones is six foot and Smith is five foot ten', do I also tell you that Jones is taller than Smith? Not in so many words, but it is implicit in what I said in the following sense: what I said entails that Jones is taller than Smith. Likewise, runs the alternative response, truth, reference and meaning are implicit in the account completed science will give of our sentence and the world in which it figures: that account will entail that the sentence is true, that it has a certain meaning, and that its parts refer to certain things, including grass. This response locates the semantic properties of sentences within the scientific account (in some wide and as yet unspecified sense of 'scientific') of sentences and the world they appear in by arguing that they are entailed by that account. The semantic gets a place in the scientific account of our world by being entailed by it.[2]

Second Example: Finding Solidity

Consider the story science tells about tables, chairs, pens, and the like being aggregations of molecules held in a lattice-like array by various intermolecular forces. Nowhere in this story is there any mention of solidity. Should we then infer that nothing is solid, or, at any rate, that anyone who thinks that the story science tells us about these dry goods is, in some strong sense, a complete story, is committed to nothing being solid? Obviously not. The story in the favoured terms will, we may suppose, tell us that these lattice-like arrays of molecules *exclude* each other, the intermolecular forces being such as to prevent the lattices encroaching on each others' spaces. And that is what it takes, according to our concept, to be solid. Or at any rate it is near enough—perhaps pre-scientifically we might have been tempted to insist that being solid required being everywhere dense in addition to resisting encroachment. But resisting encroachment explains the stubbing of toes, the supporting of cups of coffee and the like, quite well enough for it to be pedantic to insist on anything more in order to be solid.[3] Hence,

---

[2] See e.g. John Bigelow and Robert Pargetter, *Science and Necessity* (Cambridge: Cambridge University Press, 1990), 27–8.

[3] These remarks leave open whether we should identify solidity with being disposed to resist encroachment, or whether we should insist that *impenetrability* is being disposed to resist encroachment, and identify solidity with the categorical basis of impenetrability—as Rae Langton reminded me.

solidity gets a location or place in the molecular story about our world by being entailed by that story.

Serious Metaphysics: Location versus Elimination

I have just described two examples of what I mean by the location problem, and two responses that appeal to the strategy of distinguishing what is explicit in an account from what is implicit in it, in the sense of being entailed by it rather than stated in so many words. But we can generalize. Metaphysics is about what there is and what it is like. But it is not concerned with any old shopping list of what there is and what it is like. Metaphysicians seek a comprehensive account of some subject-matter—the mind, the semantic, or, most ambitiously, everything—in terms of a limited number of more or less basic notions.

John Searle objects to this kind of miserliness. For example, he objects that the debate in the philosophy of mind between dualism and monism is an absurd one. We should be *pluralists*. He observes: 'Dualists asked, "How many kinds of things . . . are there?" and counted up to two. Monists, confronting the same question, only got as far as one. *But the real mistake was to start counting at all.*'[4] Searle is right that there are lots of kinds of things. But if the thought is that any attempt to account for it all, or to account for it all as far as the mind is concerned, or to account for it all as far as the semantic is concerned, in terms of some limited set of fundamental (or more fundamental) ingredients, is mistaken in principle, then it seems to me that we are being, in effect, invited to abandon serious metaphysics in favour of drawing up big lists. What is more, we know that we can do better than draw up big lists. Some things have mass, some things have volume, and some things have density. But though density is a different property from either mass or volume (since density cannot be identified with either mass or volume), there is a clear sense in which density is not an additional feature of reality over and above mass and volume, and we can capture this by noting that the account of how things are in terms of mass and volume implicitly contains, in the sense of entailing, the account of how things are in terms of density. The same point

[4] John Searle, *The Rediscovery of the Mind* (Cambridge, Mass.: MIT Press, 1992), 26. My emphasis.

could be made with our earlier example of solidity. Solidity is not an additional feature of reality over and above the way lattice-like arrays of molecules tend to repel each other. Likewise, Jones's being taller than Smith is not a feature of how things are which is additional to Jones's being six foot and Smith's being five foot ten, if in fact Jones is six foot and Smith is five foot ten.

By serious metaphysics, I mean metaphysics inspired by these kinds of examples, metaphysics that acknowledges that we can do better than draw up big lists, that seeks comprehension in terms of a more or less limited number of ingredients, or anyway a smaller list than we started with. How big a list of basic ingredients we need, and even whether there is an ur-set, are matters open to debate; what seems to me obvious is that we can set some limits on what we need—we do not, for example, need tallness as well as the distribution of individual heights—and serious metaphysics is the investigation of where these limits should be set. Thus, by its very nature, serious metaphysics continually faces the location problem. Because the ingredients are limited, some putative features of the world are not going to appear *explicitly* in some more basic account. The question then is whether they nevertheless figure implicitly in the more basic account, or whether we should say that to accept that the account is complete, or is complete with respect to some subject-matter or other, commits us to holding that the putative features are *merely* putative. In sum, serious metaphysics is discriminatory at the same time as claiming to be complete, or complete with respect to some subject-matter, and the combination of these two features of serious metaphysics means that there are inevitably a host of putative features of our world which we must either eliminate or locate.

When does a putative feature of our world have a place in the account some serious metaphysics tells of what our world is like? I have already mentioned one answer: if the feature is entailed by the account told in the terms favoured by the metaphysics in question, it has a place in the account told in the favoured terms. This is hardly controversial considered as a sufficient condition, but, I will now argue, it is also a necessary condition: the one and only way of having a place in an account told in some set of preferred terms is by being entailed by that account—a view I will refer to as the entry by entailment thesis.

THE ENTRY BY ENTAILMENT THESIS

Physicalism as an Illustrative Example

In order to focus the discussion and set it in a familiar context, I will develop the argument for the entry by entailment thesis in terms of the particular example of physicalism and the psychological. I will argue, that is, that the psychological appears in the physicalists' account of our world if and only if that account entails the psychological account of our world. However, it will be clear, I trust, that the argument applies generally.

I start by saying something about how we should understand physicalism. Physicalism is highly discriminatory. It claims that a complete account of what our world is like, its nature (or, on some versions, a complete account of everything contingent about our world), can in principle be told in terms of a relatively small set of favoured particulars, properties, and relations, the 'physical' ones. In this sense, it is a classic example of serious metaphysics.

It is sometimes argued that physicalism is ill-defined on the ground that the key notion of a physical property or relation cannot be suitably spelt out.[5] Physicalism can be thought of as a doctrine tied especially to physics and physical chemistry, or as one tied to the physical sciences more broadly construed, including, for instance, biochemistry and genetics. In either case, runs the objection, there is a fatal unclarity about whether it is current or dreamed-of, complete-in-the-future physical science that is meant. If it is the former, physicalism is obviously false. We know here and now that current physical science—broadly or narrowly construed—is inadequate, and thus can say without further ado that any claim that a complete account of our world, or of the psychological side of our world, can be given in the terms of current physical science, must be false. While if it is the dreamed-of, complete-in-the-future physical science that is meant, physicalism

---

[5] Perhaps the most forceful, recent case for this kind of position is Tim Crane and D. H. Mellor, 'There is No Question of Physicalism', *Mind*, 99 (1990): 185–206. Incidentally, we will not be directly concerned with how one might define the notion of a physical *particular*. Our primary concern is with physicalism as a doctrine about the *kind* of world we are in. From this perspective, attribute dualism is no more physicalistically acceptable than is substantial dualism. There are various ways you might define the notion of a physical particular—object, concrete event, or whatever—in terms of the kinds of properties and relations it possesses.

is trivial. By definition, *complete* science will include all that is needed, and hence it is analytic that physicalism defined in terms of it is true. Moreover, as we do not know what the terms of this dreamed-of physical science of the future will be, a physicalism defined in terms of it is hopelessly indeterminate.

I think this problem is more apparent than real. For, first, physicalists can give an ostensive definition of what they mean by physical properties and relations by pointing to some exemplars of non-sentient objects—tables, chairs, mountains, and the like—and then say that by physical properties and relations, they mean the kinds of properties and relations needed to give a complete account of things like them. Their clearly non-trivial claim is then that the kinds of properties and relations needed to account for the exemplars of the non-sentient are enough to account for everything, or at least everything contingent.[6] There will be a problem for this way of elucidating the notion of physical properties and relations if panpsychism is true (as Ian Ravenscroft reminded me). For then there are no exemplars of the non-sentient. Everything has a mental life. But I think that we can safely set this possibility to one side.

Secondly, although this ostensive approach to the problem of identifying the intended class of physical properties and relations does not tell us which properties and relations they are, it is reasonable to suppose that physical science, despite its known inadequacies, has advanced sufficiently for us to be confident of the *kinds* of properties and relations that are needed to give a complete account of non-sentient reality. They will be broadly of a kind with those that appear in current physical science, or at least they will be as far as the explanation of macroscopic phenomena go, and the mind is a macroscopic phenomenon.[7]

Finally, physicalists can appeal to the success of micro-explanations of macroscopic phenomena. They can characterize the physical properties and relations as those that are needed to handle everything below a certain size. What this size is will be controversial given, among other things, the problems about non-locality in

[6] I am here agreeing with David Papineau, *Philosophical Naturalism* (Oxford: Basil Blackwell, 1993), 30.

[7] See e.g. J. J. C. Smart, *Our Place in the Universe* (Oxford: Basil Blackwell, 1989), 80.

quantum mechanics, but we can be reasonably confident that it will be a lot smaller than is needed for something to have psychological or semantic properties, for example.[8] This 'micro' approach does not, of course, commit physicalists to a kind of neo-Humeanism according to which a complete account of our world can be got by conjoining how things are intrinsically with relatively small bits of our world, a view which thinks of the world as a huge aggregation of parts with intrinsic natures. It may be that some of the features of the relatively small bits are irreducibly relational. On this third approach, physicalism is the clearly non-trivial claim that the kinds of properties and relations that are enough to account for everything below a certain size, and in particular below the size needed to have semantic or psychological properties, are, in suitable combinations, enough to account for everything, or anyway everything semantic and psychological.

One issue that I will set to one side is where properties like those of being a set or being a prime number figure in this classification. Some physicalists (J. J. C. Smart is an example) are happy to include them on the ground that we can be confident that any physical science of the future will need mathematics and set theory.[9] Others (David Armstrong, for example) see abstract entities and their properties as antipathetic to the essential impulse behind physicalism and seek to do without them in one way or another.[10] What is important for us is that physicalists have three reasonable things to say by way of explaining what they mean by physical properties and relations—they are those that we need to handle the non-sentient, they are broadly akin to those that appear in current physical science, they are those we need to handle the relatively small—and so have a doctrine we can understand and use as our model version of serious metaphysics.

---

[8] For a detailed defence of this approach see Philip Pettit, 'A Definition of Physicalism', *Analysis*, 53 (1993): 213–23.

[9] See e.g. Smart, *Our Place in the Universe*.

[10] D. M. Armstrong, *A Combinatorial Theory of Possibility* (Cambridge: Cambridge University Press, 1989), § 2; see also Hartry Field, *Science without Numbers* (Oxford: Basil Blackwell, 1980), and Papineau, *Philosophical Naturalism*.

[11] It may be that some of what the physicalist wants to say can be captured in

Complete Stories and Supervenience

My argument for the entry by entailment thesis as it applies to physicalism and the psychological, is that it is the physicalists' claim to have a *complete* story about the nature of our world which commits them to our world having a psychological nature if and only if that nature is entailed by the world's physical nature. Physicalism is not simply the doctrine that the world has lots of physical nature. That is not controversial: nearly everyone agrees, for instance, that objects have mass, charge, and density, and that there are gravitational and electrical force fields. The physicalists' distinctive doctrine is, as they variously say it, that the world is entirely physical in nature, that it is nothing but, or nothing over and above, the physical world, and that a full inventory of the instantiated physical properties and relations would be a full inventory *simpliciter*. What does this come to?

We can make a start by noting that one particularly clear way of showing *incompleteness* is by appeal to independent variation. What shows that three co-ordinates do not provide a complete account of location in space-time is that we can vary position in space-time while keeping any three co-ordinates constant. Hence, an obvious way to approach completeness is in terms of the *lack* of independent variation. Four co-ordinates completely specify position in space-time, because you cannot have two different positions with the same four co-ordinates. Again, a body's mass and volume completely specifies its density (or, better, its average density) because you cannot have a difference in density without a difference in at least one of mass and volume. But lack of independent variation is supervenience: position in space-time supervenes on the four co-ordinates; density supervenes on mass and volume. This suggests that we should look for a suitable supervenience thesis to capture the sense in which physicalism claims completeness.

But what sort of supervenience thesis? An *intra-world* supervenience thesis is not going to do the trick. By an intra-world supervenience thesis concerning the supervenience of, let's say, B on A, I mean a thesis of the form

> For any possible world w, if x and y are A-alike in w, then they are B-alike in w.

This intra-world supervenience thesis tells us that *as far as x and y*

are concerned, their *A*-nature secures their *B*-nature. It does *not* tell us that their *A*-nature *alone* secures their *B*-nature. For all that the intra-world thesis says, it may be that the *B*-nature of something depends on its *A*-nature along with the nature of much else besides in its world. Provided that the role of the 'much else besides' is the *same* for all *A*-alike things in that world, the intra-world supervenience thesis must come out true. Here is a simple example to illustrate the point.

> For any possible world *w*, if *x* and *y* have the same height in *w*, then *x* and *y* are alike in whether or not they are among the tallest things in *w*.

This thesis is true, but it is false that being among the tallest things is simply a matter of something's height. It is rather a matter of its height *together* with the way that its height relates to the heights of other things.

To capture physicalism's claim that the way things are, or the psychological way things are, is a matter of physical nature alone, we need to think of the supervenience base as consisting of worlds in the sense of *complete* ways things might be. For physicalism's distinctive claim is that the physical nature of our world determines the nature of our world without remainder, and we address that question via theses that say, in one form or another, that variation in the nature of a world independently of variation in the physical nature of that world is impossible. And to address this kind of question, we need to look at supervenience theses expressed in terms of quantifications over worlds, rather than in terms of quantifications over individuals in worlds. We need, that is, to look at *global* supervenience theses.[11]

As far as I can see, it does not matter for what follows precisely what ontological view among the at all plausible ones is taken of

---

the appropriate *inter*-world supervenience thesis. Thus, we might express a physicalism *about the mind* in terms of some variant of the idea that if *x* and *y* are physically exactly alike, then they are psychologically exactly alike regardless of whether they are in the same world or not, provided the worlds are alike in physical law. But issues concerning the role of a subject's environment in settling intentional content and psychological nature mean that any such strategy is bound to be controversial in ways that distract from the issue of physicalism in the wider sense that concerns us.

[12] David Lewis, *On the Plurality of Worlds* (Oxford: Basil Blackwell, 1986);

possible worlds in the sense of complete ways things might be: perhaps they are concrete entities of the same ontological type as our world, as David Lewis holds; perhaps, with the exception of our world, they are abstract entities, as Robert Stalnaker holds; perhaps (again with the exception of our world) they are structured universals, as Peter Forrest holds; perhaps (again with the exception of our world) they are certain kinds of collections—complete books or stories, say—of interpreted sentences, as Richard Jeffrey holds; perhaps the possible worlds other than ours are nothing at all, but talk of 'them' is understandable in terms of combinations of properties and relations, as David Armstrong holds.[12] I am, though, supposing that the possible-worlds way of looking at these issues is illuminating and profitable. I think the possible-worlds methodology has more than paid its dues in information science, probability and statistics, semantics, theories of representational content, decision theory, economic modelling, phase state physics, and folk speculation about possible scenarios in politics or for one's next holiday, to justify using it to illuminate issues in metaphysics. I grant that I am ducking a fundamental issue in ontology here; but to refuse to use the possible-worlds way of looking at the issues we will be concerned with because of the ontological mysteries raised by possible worlds would, it seems to me, be not that different from refusing to count one's change at the supermarket because of the ontological mysteries raised by numbers.

An example of a global supervenience thesis relating the physical way a world is to the way it is *simpliciter* is

(A) Any two possible worlds that are physical duplicates (instantiated physical property, law and relation for instantiated physical property, law and relation identical) are duplicates *simpliciter*.

But physicalism is not a claim about every possible world, but only a claim about *our* world to the effect that its physical nature exhausts all its nature. It allows, for instance, that Cartesian dualism

Robert Stalnaker, 'Possible Worlds', *Nous*, 10 (1976): 65–75; Peter Forrest, 'Ways Worlds Could Be', *Australasian Journal of Philosophy*, 64 (1986): 15–24; Richard Jeffrey, *The Logic of Decision*, 2nd edn. (Chicago, Ill.: Chicago University Press, 1983), § 12.8; and Armstrong, *A Combinatorial Theory of Possibility*.
[13] Terence Horgan, 'Supervenience and Microphysics', *Pacific Philosophical*

is true in some worlds, provided none is our world. But there is no way that (A) might be true for some hypotheses about the nature of our world and false for other hypotheses (including the hypothesis that our world is as Descartes thought). What we need in order to capture physicalism's distinctive claim, as a number of writers including Terence Horgan, David Chalmers, and David Lewis have noted, is a *contingent* global supervenience thesis:[13] a thesis that says something about the actual world and various worlds that stand in certain similarity relations to the actual world, and is contingent because its truth or falsity depends on the nature of the actual world—for some hypotheses about the nature of the actual world it comes out true, and for others it comes out false.[14] However, physicalism's claim is not that every world that is a physical duplicate of our world is a duplicate *simpliciter* of our world. Physicalists typically grant that there is a possible world physically exactly like ours but which contains as an *addition* a lot of mental life sustained in non-material stuff. Physicalism is rather the claim that if you duplicate our world in all physical respects and stop right there, you duplicate it in all respects; it says that

(B) Any world which is a *minimal* physical duplicate of our world is a duplicate *simpliciter* of our world

where a minimal physical duplicate is what you get if you 'stop right there'. (Writers of recipes and construction manuals typically

Quarterly, 63 (1982): 29–43; David Lewis, 'New Work for a Theory of Universals', *Australasian Journal of Philosophy*, 61 (1983): 343–77; and David Chalmers, *The Conscious Mind* (New York: Oxford University Press, 1996), 41–2. See also the discussion in Papineau, *Philosophical Naturalism*, and Philip Pettit, 'Microphysicalism without Contingent Micro-Macro Laws', *Analysis*, 54 (1994): 253–7.
   [14] I have often come across the following line of argument: 'Physicalism is a contingent thesis. Any global supervenience thesis leads to a *necessary* determination thesis of some kind, therefore, no global supervenience thesis captures physicalism; what's more, the whole idea of *contingent* supervenience theses is a confusion.' But in fact there is no great mystery about contingent supervenience theses: they make claims about the nature of all worlds similar in some way or other to the actual world, and the nature of appropriately similar worlds to the actual world depends in general on how things actually are. For a simple example, consider: 'Every world with exactly the same assignment of heights to exactly the same individuals as the actual world is a world in which Luc Longley is tall.' This is a true global supervenience thesis which is contingent (and *a posteriori*) because Longley might have been much shorter than he in fact is.

rely on an intuitive understanding of an implicitly included 'stop' clause in their recipes; otherwise they would face the impossible task of listing all the things you should *not* do.) Thus, a minimal physical duplicate of our world is a world that (a) is exactly like our world in every physical respect (instantiated property for instantiated property, law for law, relation for relation), and (b) contains nothing else in the sense of nothing more by way of kinds or particulars than it *must* to satisfy (a). Clause (b) is a 'no gratuitous additions' or 'stop' clause.

Thesis (B) is a claim about the nature of our world expressed in terms of a claim about a very limited range of worlds, namely the minimal physical duplicates of our world. Some physicalists want to make a bolder claim. They want to claim, for instance, that among all the worlds with the same basic laws and essentially the same ingredients as our world but maybe differently arranged and differing in number, physical nature exhausts all contingent nature, and, in particular, exhausts all psychological nature. They have to say something like: among the worlds which contain the same basic laws and ingredients as our world, any two physical duplicates are duplicates *simpliciter*.[15] But we will be concerned solely with the more restricted variety of physicalism. It will keep us busy enough, and is sufficient for our purposes.

We arrived at (B) by a rather negative path, but we can give a positive argument for the conclusion that (B) captures physicalism's essential claim. Suppose, to start with, that (B) is false. Then our world and some minimal physical duplicate of it differ; at least one contains something the other does not. But, by definition, a minimal physical duplicate of our world does not contain any laws and particulars, or instantiate any properties or relations, that do not appear in our world—everything in any minimal physical duplicate of our world is in our world. So does our world contain some laws or particulars, or instantiate some properties or relations, that the minimal physical duplicate does not? But then these particulars or properties and relations would have to be non-physical, as our world and the duplicate are physically identical, and physicalism would be false. Hence, if (B) is false, physicalism is false; that is, physicalism is committed to (B). Conversely, if

[15] For an account of this general kind, see Lewis, ' New Work for a Theory of Universals'.

physicalism is false, (B) is false. If physicalism is false, our world contains some non-physical nature in the way of particulars, laws, or instantiated properties and relations. But that nature cannot be present in any minimal physical duplicate of our world, as that nature is a non-physical addition to the physical nature of our world. But then any such world is not a duplicate *simpliciter* of our world, and, hence, (B) is false.

There are a number of issues—clarifications, possible objections, loose ends, and the like—raised by our argument that (B) captures the physicalists' essential metaphysical claim. I will address them before proceeding to give the argument that takes us from (B) to entry by entailment, but the section that follows is not essential to the overall argument. If you have no special worries about how (B) captures the physicalists' claim, you could proceed straight to the final section.

MATTERS ARISING

The Special Status of the Physical

Physicalism is associated with various asymmetry doctrines, most famously with the idea that the psychological *depends* in some sense on the physical, and not the other way around. And it is sometimes asked whether supervenience formulations of physicalism can capture the asymmetrical dependence of psychological on physical.[16] Thesis (B) passes this test. For a special case of (B) is

(B*) Any world which is a minimal physical duplicate of our world is a psychological duplicate of our world;

and the corresponding claim concerning the supervenience of the physical on the psychological is

(C) Any world which is a minimal psychological duplicate of our world is a physical duplicate of our world.

---

[16] See e.g. David Charles, 'Supervenience, Composition, and Physicalism', in David Charles and Kathleen Lennon, eds., *Reduction, Explanation, and Realism* (Oxford: Clarendon Press, 1992), 265–96, and, especially, Jaegwon Kim, '"Strong" and "Global" Supervenience Revisited', in his *Supervenience and Mind* (Cambridge: Cambridge University Press, 1993), 79–108.

It is obvious that (C) is false. It is common ground that the psychological grossly underdetermines the physical. For the physicalist, the asymmetry between physical and psychological (or semantic, or economic, or biological, . . .) lies in the fact that the physical fully determines the psychological (or semantic, . . .), whereas the psychological (or semantic, . . .) grossly underdetermines the physical. In the same way, the full account of who is tall grossly underdetermines individual heights, whereas the full account of the distribution of individual heights fully determines who is tall; this is the sense in which tallness depends on individual heights, but not conversely.

Necessary Connections between Distinct Properties

It might be objected that physical properties are necessarily connected to non-physical properties, and so any minimal physical duplicate of our world is bound to have some non-physical nature. For instance, having mass is a physical property—we need it to account for the non-sentient, and it (or some near relative) will surely have a place in completed physics—but it is necessarily connected to having mass or being made of ectoplasm, and having mass or being made of ectoplasm is not a physical property.[17]

To address this objection, I need to say something about our use of the term 'property' (and 'relation', but, as the issues are essentially the same, I'll suppress this complication in what follows), and something about our use of the term 'non-physical'. When I talk of properties in this chapter and the chapters that follow, I am not entering the debate in analytic ontology between, for instance, platonic realism and resemblance nominalism over the problem of the one and the many. I am simply supposing that predicates apply in virtue of how things are; if a predicate applies to one thing and not to another, this is because of something about how the two things are over and above the fact that the predicate applies to one and not the other. This supervenience of predication on nature is required for predicates to serve the purpose of saying how things are. Property talk, as we will be understanding it, is a way of

---

[17] Where ectoplasm is to be understood as a kind of stuff incompatible with the physicalists' view of what kinds there are—perhaps the stuff out of which thoughts are made according to Descartes.

talking of the nature on which predication supervenes: thus, 'being *F*' or 'the property of being *F*' picks out the nature in virtue of which '*F*' applies. Platonic realism, a sparse non-platonic or Aristotelian realism of the kind advanced by David Armstrong, resemblance nominalism, and so on and so forth, are then various doctrines about how to spell out (in inevitably controversial detail) exactly what is involved in the supervenience of predication on nature.[18]

Our notion of properties—properties-in-nature, we might call them—is to be distinguished from the notion of properties allied to concepts or predicate meanings. The notion we need in discussing metaphysical theses in speculative cosmology like physicalism is the properties-in-nature one, for these theses are precisely views about what the world is like.[19] Also, our properties-in-nature need not be particularly *natural*. Fish and fowl have something in common over and above the fact that the predicate 'is a fish or a fowl' applies to them but the something in common is not particularly natural.

By a *non-physical* property, I mean one whose instantiation is inconsistent with physicalism. The debate over physicalism is best thought of as operating with a *tripartite* division of properties. There is the list of physicalism's preferred properties picked out in one of the three ways discussed earlier, or in some suitable variant on them. These are the physical properties. Then there are the properties whose instantiation is inconsistent with physicalism, for instance, as we recently supposed, the property of being made of ectoplasm. These are the non-physical properties. Finally, there are the properties that are onlookers in the debate over physicalism, properties whose instantiation can be accepted by both sides in the debate. Thus, 'non-physical property' in the debate over physicalism does *not* mean 'property that is not physical'. This is an unfortunate terminological fact, but the debate is too far along to switch to a better term like, say, 'anti-physical'.

[18] See D. M. Armstrong, *Universals and Scientific Realism*, 2 vols. (Cambridge: Cambridge University Press, 1978), for discussion of the various views in analytic ontology as well as a defence of his own account. For the supervenience of predication on nature, see Bigelow and Pargetter, *Science and Necessity*, 93–4. I will also sometimes talk of the way things are making, or failing to make, sentences true and predicates apply, to use the terms we owe to C. B. Martin.

[19] The bearing of this conception of properties on the issue of whether there are necessarily co-extensive but distinct properties is addressed in Chapter 5.

Now, having mass or being made of ectoplasm is in the third, onlooker, category. For it can be possessed in two different ways, namely, by having mass—the way it is possessed in our world according to physicalists; and by being made of ectoplasm—a way it is never possessed in our world according to physicalists (and nearly everyone) but a way it is sometimes possessed in the world according to Descartes. Thus its possession, in and of itself, does not imply anything one way or the other concerning the truth of physicalism.

We can now give the reply to the objection from necessary connections between properties. None of the plausible examples of necessary connections from physical properties to distinct properties that are not physical properties is an example of a connection from a physical to a non-physical property. They are all like our example of having mass and having mass or ectoplasm: the necessary connections are between physical properties and onlooker properties.

Supervenience and Singular Thought[20]

To accept (B) is *ipso facto* to accept, as we noted earlier,

  (B*) Any world which is a minimal physical duplicate of our world is a psychological duplicate of our world.

Consider a minimal physical duplicate of the actual world. It will contain a duplicate of Bush. It might be urged that our Bush's psychology, while being very similar to his duplicate's, will not be quite the same as his duplicate's. Their singular thoughts will be different by virtue of being directed to different objects. Only our Bush is thinking about our Clinton. Thus, if physicalism is committed to (B*), physicalism is false.

One response to this putative disproof of physicalism would be to challenge the view about singular thought that lies behind it, but I think we can steer clear of that issue for our purposes here. The disproof is put in terms that trade on the counterpart way of thinking about objects in possible worlds: the way according to which no object appears in more than one world, and what makes

---

[20] I am indebted to Rae Langton and David Lewis in what follows.

it the case that an object which is *F* might have failed to be *F* is the fact that its counterpart in some possible world is not *F*.[21] However, the duplicate of our Bush is thinking about the very same person as our Bush in the only sense that the counterpart theorist can take seriously. If I had scratched my nose a moment ago, I would still have had the very same nose that I actually have. Noses are not that easy to remove and replace. The counterpart theorist has to say that what makes that true are certain facts about the nose of my counterpart in a world where my counterpart scratched his nose a moment ago. If that is good enough for being the very same nose, then the corresponding facts about Bush's counterpart are good enough for it to be true that he is thinking about the very same person, and hence having the same singular thought.

The putative disproof might, though, be developed without trading on the counterpart way of thinking about these matters. A believer in trans-world identity typically holds that whether an object in our world is literally identical with an object in another is not a qualitative matter. Such a theorist might well hold that although Bush, our Bush, and Clinton, our Clinton, eyeball each other in more worlds than this one, it is nevertheless true that in some minimal physical duplicates of our world, our Bush thinks about a qualitative duplicate of our Clinton who, nevertheless, is not our Clinton—there is a *haecceitic* difference, a difference in 'thisness'. On some views about singular thought, Bush will count as having a different thought in such a world from the thought he has in our world. In this case the 'steering clear' requires a modification of (B). The physicalist will need to require that minimal physical duplicates of our world be ones which, in addition to being identical in respect of physical properties, laws, and relations with our world, are identical in which *haecceities* are associated with which physical properties, laws, and relations.

Egocentric Claims and De Se Content

We have beliefs and make claims about how things are in general, about, that is, how the world is. We can think of these as *de dicto* beliefs and assertions. Thus, I might believe or claim that there are

---

[21] See Lewis, *On the Plurality of Worlds*, § 1. 2.

tigers somewhere or other. We also have beliefs and make claims about how things are with us. We can think of these as egocentric or *de se* beliefs and assertions. Thus, I might believe or assert that there are tigers near *me*. The evolutionary significance of egocentric or *de se* beliefs and assertions is obvious: that there are tigers and that there is water is important; where in space and time the tigers and water are with respect to oneself is especially important.

There is a sense in which egocentric assertions and beliefs have a perspective or point of view built into them, for they make claims about how things are with, or from the perspective of, the producer of the sentence and the holder of the belief. However, the physical story about our world is, as has often been emphasized, a perspective-free account of our world—or, as it is sometimes called, an absolute conception of the world.[22] A fair question, therefore, is whether noting the phenomenon of egocentric content gives us an immediate reason to deny the kind of physicalism expressed by (B).[23] It might well be asked: How could the truth or falsity of egocentric beliefs and assertions supervene on a story about physical nature alone, in view of the perspective-free nature of any physical story?

One way to tackle this question is to attempt a reduction of egocentric or *de se* content to the non-egocentric or *de dicto*: to urge that claims and beliefs about how things are with the claimer or believer can invariably be translated in some way or other into how things are with the world. For my part, I have been convinced by the arguments of, among others, Hector-Neri Castañeda, John Perry, and David Lewis, that egocentric or *de se* content is irreducibly so.[24] Nevertheless, I do not think that the irreducibility of egocentric content raises any special problem for physicalism.

---

[22] See e.g. Bernard Williams, *Ethics and the Limits of Philosophy* (London: Fontana, 1985), ch. 8.

[23] There have, of course, been considerations other than those explicitly turning on egocentric content advanced in support of the idea that a perspective-free account of the world is impossible, and so that any absolute conception of the world, including physicalism, is bound to be incomplete. See e.g. the later sections of Thomas Nagel, 'What is it Like to be a Bat?', *Philosophical Review*, 83 (1974): 435–50. Some of the issues are further explored in his *The View from Nowhere* (New York: Oxford University Press, 1986). What I say above does not bear on these other arguments, except to the extent that they turn implicitly on the existence of egocentric content.

[24] John Perry, 'The Problem of the Essential Indexical', *Nous*, 13 (1979): 3–21; Hector-Neri Castañeda, '*He: A Study in the Logic of Self-Consciousness', *Ratio*, 8

The physicalist can appeal to (a) the fact that there is a *context* for any and every utterance of a sentence, or holding of a belief, with *de se* or egocentric content, and (b) the way that this context operates to ensure that the nature of the world determines without remainder the truth or falsity of token sentences and beliefs with egocentric content: because any and every token with *de se* content has a context, its truth-value is fully determined by the *de dicto* account of how things are, despite the fact that *de se* content is not reducible to *de dicto* content.

We can illustrate the point with the kind of example used to show the irreducibility of *de se* content to *de dicto* content. Consider a world consisting of two qualitatively identical epochs, each containing one person called Jones. Both Joneses might know all there is to know about what the world is like, including its repeated nature, and yet, on the sensible ground that they know that they have no way of telling one epoch from the other, fail to have any belief about which epoch they are in. They each believe, let's say, that they live in a country called 'Iceland', but do not have any belief about whether it is the Iceland in the first epoch or the Iceland in the second epoch which they inhabit. Now suppose that each comes—rashly and irrationally, presumably—to believe that she herself is in the first epoch. This they can do without their *de dicto* beliefs changing in any way. But then what they each come to believe about their own location in the first epoch cannot be reduced to their *de dicto* beliefs about what their world is like. For their *de se* beliefs have changed, whereas their *de dicto* ones have remained exactly as before. In the same way, we might suppose that each comes to assert that she herself is in the first epoch, and a similar argument shows that their rash *de se* assertions are not reducible to *de dicto* claims. Now what the physicalist can say about these *de se* beliefs and assertions is that for each rash *token* with the content that she herself is in the first epoch, its truth or falsity is fully determined by how the world in question is. This is because the tokens have a context. Thus, the first Jones's belief and claim is by someone in the first epoch, and so is true if and only if—*de dicto* fact—the first Jones is in the first epoch, and, accordingly, both belief and assertion are true. The second Jones's belief and

(1966): 130–57; and David Lewis, 'Attitudes *De Dicto* and *De Se*', *Philosophical Review*, 88 (1979): 513–43.

claim is by someone in the second epoch, and so is true if and only if—*de dicto* fact—the second Jones is in the first epoch, and, accordingly, both belief and assertion are false. This does not mean that we are going back on the irreducibility of *de se* content. Although an alert Jones will know that the truth or falsity of her belief and assertion that she herself is in the first epoch are determined without remainder by the *de dicto* nature of the world, that fact does not tell her whether she is the first or second Jones, and so does not tell her *which way* the *de dicto* story about the world determines the truth, or determines the falsity, of her belief and assertion. Her rash *de se* belief and assertion will still outrun her *de dicto* beliefs and assertions about her world. A similar point applies to the famous example of the insomniac who believes that it is now 3 a.m. This belief is not equivalent to any belief expressible in terms of dates and times, but each and every token of a belief with the content that it is now 3 a.m. will have a location in time givable in terms of dates and times, and in consequence will be true just if the time in the relevant date and time specification is 3 a.m.

In sum, the truth-value of each and every token with egocentric or *de se* content supervenes on the full *de dicto* story about the world, and hence there is no quick refutation of physicalism as captured by (B) from the conjunction of the existence of egocentric or *de se* content with the perspective-free nature of the physical account of the world.

It might be objected that this argument merely shows that the existence of egocentric content does not reveal the incompleteness of the physicalist's account of *what the world is like*; it says nothing about what the physicalist should say about the content of an assertion like that *I myself* weigh 75 kilos, an assertion that is irreducibly about me and not equivalent to any statement entirely about what the world is like. But the content of such an assertion is simply the property ascribed, which in this case is the transparently physical one of weighing 75 kilos. In other cases the physicalist will have substantial work to do to show that the property ascribed is physical (or is an onlooker) property, but egocentric content in itself is not a problem, or so it seems to me.[25]

---

[25] Lewis shows how to treat *all* content as self-ascription of properties in 'Attitudes *De Dicto* and *De Se*'.

Indeterminacy

The next 'matter arising' concerns the fact that the physical story about our world will be much more determinate than the story told in various non-physical terms. There is much more indeterminacy, for instance, about when the world started coming out of the recession of the 1930s, or where in the chain of being, rational thought starts, than there is about how much I weigh, or how many electrons there are. Here, the physicalist must allow that one way of being exactly alike is by being exactly alike in what is indeterminate. A similar sort of understanding is called for when we construe the supervenience of baldness on hair distribution. Baldness is a much more indeterminate matter than is hair distribution, nevertheless baldness is nothing over and above hair distribution (considered globally; there is a comparative element involved in being bald). Thus, if we wish to capture this fact in a supervenience thesis, we must allow that one way that worlds exactly alike in hair distribution are exactly alike in baldness distribution is by being alike in the cases where it is indeterminate whether or not we have baldness.

Necessary Beings

Some theists believe that God exists necessarily and has all sorts of properties that rule God out as part of the physical picture of what our world is like. If they also hold that God is the *only* exception to physicalism—the world apart from God is indeed entirely physical—they will accept (B). But surely they do not count as physicalists.

The problem here is distinct from that raised by allegedly necessary beings like numbers and sets. It is (as we noted earlier) arguable, and in any case not something we will be contesting, that numbers and sets count as physical on the ground that they have a place in physical science via their place in mathematics. But the necessary being that some theists believe in has properties that have no place in physical science.

You might reply by saying that the sense in which God is a necessary being is metaphysical, and the sense in which the worlds we quantify over in (B) are possible is conceptual, but for reasons that will become apparent in Chapter 3, *I* cannot say this. For in that chapter I argue against the way of looking at the metaphysical/conceptual necessity distinction implicit in this reply.

You might reply by urging that a *minimal* physical duplicate of our world would, according to these theists, not be a duplicate *simpliciter* of our world, because it would not contain God. But a minimal physical duplicate of our world means, and has to mean, a duplicate that contains only what it *must* in order to be a physical duplicate, and, according to these theists, every world must contain God, and so *a fortiori* every physical duplicate must contain God.

What the physicalist has to say, it seems to me, is that there is a distinction between capturing the content of a doctrine, and capturing the content of a doctrine in a way that will satisfy everyone *regardless of what else they believe*. The latter task is impossible. After all, if people have inconsistent views, anything you say will, when combined with what else they believe, entail any and everything! The theists in question have, the physicalist must say, inconsistent views—the kind of necessary being theists believe in is impossible. It is not obviously impossible, of course. If it were, there would be very few theists of this necessary stripe. What physicalists are offering when they put forward (B) is an account of the content of physicalism for those with consistent views.

Kantian Physicalism

When physicists tell us about the properties they take to be fundamental, they tell us about what these properties *do*. This is no accident. We know about what things are like essentially through the way they impinge on us and on our measuring instruments. It does not follow from this that the fundamental properties of current physics, or of 'completed' physics, are causal cum relational ones. It may be that our terms for the fundamental properties pick out the properties they do via the causal relations the properties enter into, but that at least some of the properties so picked out are intrinsic. They have, as we might put it, relational names but intrinsic essences. However, it does suggest the possibility that (i) there are two quite different intrinsic properties, P and P^*, which are exactly alike in the causal relations they enter into, (ii) sometimes one is possessed and sometimes the other, and (iii) we mistakenly think that there is just one property because the difference does not make a difference (as the point is put in information theory). An obvious extension of this possibility leads to the un-comfortable idea that we may know next to nothing about the in-trinsic nature of our world. We know only its causal cum relational nature. One way to block this result is to deny that there can be distinct properties with identical causal profiles. If they have iden-tical causal profiles, 'they' are one and the same property.[26] This, to my way of thinking, is too close to holding that the nature of everything is relational cum causal, which makes a mystery of what it is that stands *in* the causal relations. I think we should ac-knowledge as a possible, interesting position one we might call Kantian physicalism. It holds that a large part (possibly all) of the intrinsic nature of our world is irretrievably beyond our reach, but that all the nature we know about supervenes on the (mostly or entirely) causal cum relational nature that the physical sciences tell us about. If Kantian physicalism is true, some minimal physical duplicates of our world differ markedly from our world in intrinsic nature, but not in ways that the inhabitants of those worlds know about—the 'pains' are just as painful, the 'water' is just as refresh-ing, the 'beliefs' respond to the impact of sensory information and move bodies around in exactly the same ways, and so on. I will conduct the discussion to follow in terms of physicalism as tradi-tionally understood, but it seems to me that much of what I say could be framed equally in terms of Kantian physicalism.

It is time to return to the main plot.

THE PATH TO ENTRY BY ENTAILMENT

It is easy to show, given that (B) follows from physicalism, that if physicalism is true, then the psychological account of our world is entailed by the physical account of our world.[27] For it follows from (B) that any psychological sentence about our world is en-tailed by the physical nature of our world.

---

[26] See e.g. Sydney Shoemaker, 'Causality and Properties', in his *Identity, Cause, and Mind* (Cambridge: Cambridge University Press, 1984), 206–33.

[27] For an early version of the argument that follows, though set in a different framework, see Robert Kirk, 'From Physical Explicability to Full Blooded Materialism', *Philosophical Quarterly*, 29 (1979): 229–37.

Let Φ be the story as told in purely physical terms, which is true at the actual world and all the minimal physical duplicates of the actual world, and false elsewhere; Φ is a hugely complex, purely physical account of our world. Let Ψ be any true sentence which is about the psychological nature of our world in the sense that it can only come false by things being different psychologically from the way they actually are: every world at which Ψ is false differs in some psychological way from our world. Intuitively, the idea is that Ψ counts as being about the psychological nature of our world because making it false requires supposing a change in the distribution of psychological properties and relations. Now if (B) is true, every world at which Φ is true is a duplicate *simpliciter* of our world, and so *a fortiori* a psychological duplicate of our world. But then every world at which Φ is true is a world at which Ψ is true—that is, Φ entails Ψ.[28]

There is, of course, another use of the term 'entails', sometimes tagged 'conceptually entails' or '*a priori* entails', according to which Φ entails Ψ only if Ψ is *a priori* deducible from Φ. So I should emphasize that by 'entails' here I mean simply the necessary truth-preserving notion—call it 'necessary determination' or 'fixing' if you prefer. I address the issue of the connection between the doctrine that the physical account entails—necessarily determines, fixes—the psychological account, with the doctrine that the physical account enables the *a priori* deduction of the psychological account at the end of Chapter 3.

Also, when I say that Φ is a sentence, I mean that it is a sentence in some idealized language constructed from the materials that serve to give the full, complete account of the physical sciences—or of physics itself, if we have in mind a version of physicalism tied to physics rather than the physical sciences in general. We cannot actually construct Φ because we do not and never will know enough, and even if we did know enough, the task of writing or uttering Φ would be completely beyond our powers. It might be

---

[28] What about sentences with egocentric content? We can think of a purely physical story as being in part about the physical nature of an individual as well as being about the physical nature of a world—thus the story might include, as we noted earlier, that I myself weigh 75 kilos—and by an obvious extension of the argument in the text, the physicalist must hold that the relevant egocentric psychological story about, say, me, is, if true, entailed by the relevant purely physical story about me as well as about the world.

objected that this means that we do not really understand what physicalism is committed to. But consider the (true) sentence in English, 'The average size of houses in 1990 is under 1,000 square metres.' We know that this sentence is entailed by a very long conjunction made up of conjuncts of the form '— is a house in 1990 of such and such a size' together with a conjunct that says how many houses there are, in an idealized version of English with distinct names for every distinct house. Despite the fact that we will never go close to writing down this sentence, we understand perfectly well what has just been claimed—as is evidenced by the fact that we know that it is true.

Finally, Φ must contain some such clause as 'and that is all'—the 'stop' clause—in order to be true only at minimal physical duplicates of the actual world. So when I say physicalists are committed to the story about our world as told in purely physical terms entailing *inter alia* its psychological nature, I am ruling that a clause like 'and that is all' when attached to a purely physical story preserves its purely physical character. Those unhappy with this ruling will have to say that physicalists are committed to the story about our world as told in purely physical terms (except for the stop clause) entailing *inter alia* its psychological nature.

We have now derived the entry by entailment thesis for the special case of physicalism and the psychological. A putative psychological fact has a place in the physicalists' world view if and only if it is entailed by Φ. Any putative psychological fact which is not so entailed must be regarded by the physicalist as either a refutation of physicalism or as *merely* putative. Moreover, although the argument was developed for the special case of physicalism and the psychological, the argument did not depend crucially on matters local to that special case. We could have argued in the same general way in the case of physicalism and the semantic, or in the case of Cartesian dualism and the semantic, or in the case of Berkeleyan idealism and physical objects. Our argument essentially turned on just two facts about any serious metaphysics or piece of speculative cosmology: it is discriminatory, and it claims completeness. It is these two features of serious metaphysics, combined with the account of completeness in terms of supervenience and the way the truth-conditions of sentences can be represented in terms of possible worlds, which mean that serious metaphysics is committed to views about which sentences entail which other sentences.

How does the entry by entailment thesis show the importance of conceptual analysis? That is the business of the next chapter.

CHAPTER 2

The Role of Conceptual Analysis

IN the first chapter we noted that serious metaphysics is discriminatory at the same time as aspiring to completeness concerning some subject-matter or other (or, in its most ambitious manifestations, everything). In consequence, it is committed to global supervenience theses and, thereby, to entailment theses. In particular, I argued that one well-known manifestation of serious metaphysics, physicalism, is committed to showing that sentences about the psychological way things are are entailed by sentences about the physical way things are.

The purpose of this chapter is to draw the connection with conceptual analysis. I offer an answer to the question: Why should a commitment to entailment theses between matters described in some preferred vocabulary and matters described in various other vocabularies require serious metaphysicians to do conceptual analysis?

The short answer is that conceptual analysis is the very business of addressing when and whether a story told in one vocabulary is made true by one told in some allegedly more fundamental vocabulary. When Roderick Chisholm and A. J. Ayer analysed knowledge as true justified belief, they were offering an account of what makes an account of how things are told using the word 'knowledge' true in terms of an account using the terms 'true', 'justified', and 'belief'. It counted as a piece of conceptual analysis because it was intended to survive the method of possible cases. They sought to deliver an account of when various possible cases should be described as cases of knowledge that squared with our clear intuitions. And, of course, they failed. Edmund Gettier described certain possible cases of true by accident but nevertheless justified belief, and invited us to agree with his intuition that they should not be described as cases of knowledge.[1] We accepted his invita-

---

[1] Edmund Gettier, 'Is Justified True Belief Knowledge?', *Analysis*, 23 (1963):

tion and the analysis of knowledge merry-go-round started. Likewise, Hilary Putnam and Saul Kripke refuted at least some (*some*) versions of the description theory of reference by appeal to intuitions about possible cases.[2] They described cases where all the descriptions required for a term *T* to refer to object *O* according to certain versions of the description theory were satisfied by *O*, and yet intuition refused to assent to the view that *O* was in fact what was referred to by *T*.

In this chapter I give the longer answer. I elaborate the picture just sketched in a way designed to make clear its plausible theoretical underpinnings, and to meet some of the many objections that so many now have to conceptual analysis. As in the first chapter, the example of physicalism and the psychological will be appealed to at various points.

THE THEORETICAL RATIONALE FOR CONCEPTUAL ANALYSIS

Avoiding Acts of Faith

If some variety of serious metaphysics is committed to an account of how things are in one vocabulary being made true by how things are as told in some other vocabulary, it had better have to hand an account of how accounts in the two vocabularies are interconnected. For instance, physicalists who are not eliminativists about intentional states have to say *something* about how the physical story about our world makes true the intentional story about it. Otherwise their realism about intentional states will be more an act of faith than anything else. For they will have nothing to say to one who insists that their view that a complete account of the nature of our world can be given in purely physical terms without recourse to intentional vocabulary is precisely the view that there are no intentional states. They will, that is, have nothing to

121–3. He addresses the versions of the true justified belief account in Roderick M. Chisholm, *Perceiving* (Ithaca, NY: Cornell University Press, 1957), and A. J. Ayer, *The Problem of Knowledge* (London: Macmillan, 1956). The versions are slightly different but in ways that are irrelevant to Gettier's counter-examples.

   [2] Saul Kripke, *Naming and Necessity* (Oxford: Basil Blackwell, 1980); Hilary Putnam, 'The Meaning of "Meaning"', in his *Language, Mind and Reality* (Cambridge: Cambridge University Press, 1975).

say to justify calling themselves realists rather than eliminativists about intentional states. Of course, some physicalists are happy to embrace eliminativism about intentional states, or to take a 'don't care' attitude to the debate between realism and eliminativism about intentional states. Paul Churchland is an example of the first, and perhaps Daniel Dennett is an example of the second.[3] But I doubt if there are any physicalists happy to embrace eliminativism about, or to take a don't care attitude to, *everything* as described in a vocabulary other than the austere physical one. Surely it is beyond serious question that at least some of: rivers, inflation, explosions, buildings, and wars exist. Some existential claims expressed in a language other than the austerely physical are true. It follows that every physicalist must address the making-true question at some stage or other.

But why suppose that the interesting account that physicalists must give of how and why the physical account of our world makes true the psychological account (or the economic or the geographical or . . .) of our world must involve conceptual analysis? The answer to this question turns on the importance of defining one's subject, and a certain view about what is involved in doing this.

Defining the Subject

Although metaphysics is about what the world is like, the *questions* we ask when we do metaphysics are framed in a language, and thus we need to attend to what the users of the language mean by the words they employ to ask their questions. When bounty hunters go searching, they are searching for a person and not a handbill. But they will not get very far if they fail to attend to the representational properties of the handbill on the wanted person. These properties give them their target, or, if you like, define the subject of their search. Likewise, metaphysicians will not get very far with questions like: Are there Ks? Are Ks nothing over and above Js? and, Is the K way the world is fully determined by the J

---

[3] See e.g. Paul Churchland, 'Eliminative Materialism and the Propositional Attitudes', *Journal of Philosophy*, 78 (1981): 67–90, and Daniel C. Dennett, *Consciousness Explained* (Boston, Mass.: Little Brown & Co., 1991), 'Appendix A (For Philosophers)'.

way the world is? in the absence of some conception of what counts as a *K*, and what counts as a *J*.

How then should we go about defining our subject *qua* metaphysicians when we ask about *K*s for some *K*-kind of interest to us? It depends on what we are interested in doing. If I say that what *I* mean—never mind what others mean—by a free action is one such that the agent would have done otherwise if he or she had chosen to, then the existence of free actions so conceived will be secured, and so will the compatibility of free action with determinism. If I say that what *I* mean—never mind what others mean—by 'belief' is any information-carrying state that causes subjects to utter sentences like 'I believe that snow is white', the existence of beliefs so conceived will be safe from the eliminativists' arguments. But in neither case will I have much of an audience. I have turned interesting philosophical debates into easy exercises in deductions from stipulative definitions together with accepted facts.

What then are the interesting philosophical questions that we are seeking to address when we debate the existence of free action and its compatibility with determinism, or about eliminativism concerning intentional psychology? What we are seeking to address is whether free action *according to our ordinary conception*, or something suitably close to our ordinary conception, exists and is compatible with determinism, and whether intentional states *according to our ordinary conception*, or something suitably close to it, will survive what cognitive science reveals about the operations of our brains.

The Role of Intuitions about Possible Cases

But how should we identify our ordinary conception? The only possible answer, I think, is by appeal to what seems to us most obvious and central about free action, determinism, belief, or whatever, as revealed by our intuitions about possible cases. Intuitions about how various cases, including various merely possible cases, are correctly described in terms of free action, determinism, and belief are precisely what reveal our ordinary conceptions of free action, determinism, and belief, or, as it is often put nowadays, our folk theory of them. For what guides me in describing an action as free is revealed by my intuitions about whether various possible cases are or are not cases of free action. Thus my intuitions about possible cases reveal my theory of free action—they could hardly be supposed to reveal someone else's! Likewise, your intuitions reveal your theory. To the extent that our intuitions coincide, they reveal our shared theory. To the extent that our intuitions coincide with those of the folk, they reveal the folk theory. Thus the general coincidence in intuitive responses to the Gettier examples reveals something about the folk theory of knowledge in the sense of revealing what governs folk ascriptions of knowledge.[4] I have occasionally come across people who resolutely resist the Gettier cases. Sometimes it has seemed right to accuse them of confusion—they haven't properly understood the cases, or they haven't seen the key similarities to other cases where they accept that subjects do not know, or the key differences from cases they accept as cases of knowledge—but sometimes it is clear that they are not confused; what we then learn from the stand-off is simply that they use the word 'knowledge' to cover different cases from most of us. In these cases it is, it seems to me, misguided to accuse them of error (unless they go on to say that their concept of knowledge is ours), though they are, of course, missing out on an interesting way of grouping together cases—the way we effect with the term 'knowledge'—that cuts across the grouping effected in terms of true justified belief, and which has its own distinctive role to play in epistemology.

Extracting a person's theory of what counts as a K from intuitions about how to describe possible cases, and taking it to reveal their concept of K-hood, is not a peculiarly philosophical business. Child psychologists are interested in what young children understand by 'x goes faster than y', and they argue from the fact that, up to a certain age, children say that x goes faster than y whenever x gets to some designated destination before y, regardless of where x and y start from, that young children's concept of *faster than* is

---

[4] I here take the controversial view that folk conceptions should be thought of as amalgams of individual conceptions. Thus, my intuitions reveal the folk conception in as much as I am reasonably entitled, as I usually am, to regard myself as typical. But the argument to follow does not depend on taking the order of determination to be from individual to folk. It depends on taking intuitions about possible cases to reveal folk conceptions—and it is hard to see how this could be denied except by taking the view that it is better to say what is counterintuitive than what is intuitive.

our adult concept of *getting there before*. (Speaking as an amateur, I confess that the evidence they cite seems to point more towards the view that the children's concept is indeterminate between *getting there before* and *faster than;* the reasons they cite for eliminating the hypothesis that the children's concept is the same as ours but they do not know how to allow for differences in starting-place, seem to me to point towards a failure to grasp our distinction between the two concepts. But the key point for us is the centrality of responses to cases in elucidating concepts, for non-philosophers as well as philosophers, rather than how well the method has been followed in this case.) Political scientists, and many folk if it comes to that, infer that a typical American voter's concept of *socialist* is very different from that of a typical French or British voter, precisely from the difference in the cases—policies, people, or whatever—that American as opposed to French and British voters describe as socialist. The business of consulting intuitions about possible cases is simply part of the overall business of elucidating concepts by determining how subjects classify possibilities. It is that part of the business that costs less than setting up the experiments, and also that part of the business that is practicable when dealing with cases that are merely possible and cannot be set up in practice like, famously, Twin Earth.

To avoid misunderstanding, I should enter an explanation, and make two disclaimers at this stage. The explanation concerns my use of the word 'concept'. Our subject is really the elucidation of the possible situations covered by the *words* we use to ask our questions—concerning free action, knowledge, and the relation between the physical and the psychological, or whatever. I use the word 'concept' partly in deference to the traditional terminology which talks of *conceptual* analysis, and partly to emphasize that though our subject is the elucidation of the various situations covered by bits of language according to one or another language user, or by the folk in general, it is divorced from considerations local to any particular language. When we ask English users in English for their intuitive responses to whether certain cases are or are not cases of knowledge, we get information (fallible information, more on this later) about the cases they do and do not count as covered by the English word 'knowledge'. But our focus is on getting clear about the cases covered rather than on what does the covering, the word *per se*. We mark this by talking of conceptual analysis rather than word or sentence analysis. Moreover, although our focus is on getting clear about the cases covered, this does not commit us to the view that necessary co-extension is the criterion of concept identity. We can agree, for instance, that on one acceptable use of the term 'concept', *equilateral triangle* is not the same concept as *equiangular triangle,* despite the fact that every possible case covered by the one is covered by the other. For we can draw the desired distinction in terms of the possibilities' framework. We are free to regard the first as a compound concept containing the constituent concept *equilateral* in the place where the second contains the concept *equiangular*; they can then be counted as different in view of the fact that these constituent concepts are *not* necessarily co-extensive. The position would be simply an obvious extension of the way Carnapian intensional isomorphism is distinguished from synonymy.[5]

Secondly, I should emphasize that I am not seeking to revive the paradigm case argument.[6] It is no part of the view being defended here that the cases from which one learns or acquires a concept or term must fall under that concept or term. One might be presented with cases that one takes to have a certain feature, and resolve, or learn, or be told, or agree, to use *T* for cases that have this feature; that is, to use *T* for the feature. Nothing about this procedure entails that the original cases actually have the feature. Also, we often learn to use a term by being presented with cases that are given to us as ones the term does *not* apply to, but which naturally suggest to us the cases to which the term does apply. Most of us learned the term 'tiger' in this way (it is safer than confrontation with the real thing). Also, many theoretical terms like 'acid', 'kinetic energy', 'fish', and 'acacia' are ones whose extension is in part determined by the nature of the best, true theory in which the term appears. To take Michael Slote's example, the reason a whale does not count as a fish is not that we happened to settle on a list of cri-

---

[5] See e.g. David Lewis, 'General Semantics', reprinted in his *Philosophical Papers*, vol. i (New York: Oxford University Press, 1983). We will see later, in the discussion of the distinction between *A*-extensions and *C*-extensions, how the difference between the concept *water* and the concept H_2O might be distinguished in terms of possibilities, despite the fact that every possible case of water is a case of H_2O, and conversely.

[6] I am indebted here to a discussion with Georges Rey, and throughout this section to discussions with Jonathan Berg, but they should not be held responsible.

teria for being a fish that included trout and excluded whales. Rather, it is an implicit part of serious classificatory practice that we seek to mark the divisions worth marking, and when biological science told us which features were important for dividing fish from mammals—having gills is more important than here and now living in water, for instance—this meant that trout counted as fish, and whales counted as mammals.[7] In the case of a theoretical term like this, before we know what the best theory says (and, of course, sometimes we never know what the best theory says; it forever eludes us), we have no paradigm cases for the term. It might be thought that we will not be able to give necessary and sufficient conditions for K-hood in such cases before the relevant theory is with us. (Slote seems to think this, though the matter is not entirely clear to me.) But all that follows is that we need to state them in long disjunctions of longish conjunctions of the following kind: x is a fish if and only if (the best true theory in biology says that the important properties out of or descended from or explanatory of F_1, F_2, F_3, . . . are so-and-so, and x has so-and-so) or (the best true theory in biology says that the important properties out of or descended from or explanatory of F_1, F_2, F_3, . . . are such-and-such, and x has such-and-such) or . . ., where F_1, F_2, F_3, . . . are the properties we initially associate with being a fish (the properties of the exemplars). Or, for short, x is a fish iff x has the important properties out of or descended from or explanatory of F_1, F_2, F_3, . . ., according to the best true theory.

Also, following on from the point just made, we should note that the method of possible cases needs to be applied with some sophistication. A person's first-up response as to whether something counts as a K may well need to be discounted. One or more of: the theoretical role they give K-hood, evidence concerning other cases they count as instances of K, signs of confused thinking on their part, cases where their classification is, on examination, a derivative one (they say it's a K because it is very obviously a J, and they think, defeasibly, that any J is a K), their readiness to back off under questioning, and the like, can justify rejecting a subject's first-up classifications as revealing their concept of K-hood. We noted this point in our discussion of whether child psychologists

[7] Michael Slote, 'The Theory of Important Criteria', *Journal of Philosophy*, 63 (1966): 211–24.

are right to infer that young children's concept of *faster than* is ours of *getting there before*; we observed that exactly what should be inferred from the young children's responses is not transparent. And an example familiar to every epistemologist is provided by the Gettier cases. Many philosophers classified cases of true justified belief as cases of knowledge, convinced that they were so classifying them precisely because they were cases of true justified belief. Reflection on the Gettier cases showed them that they were wrong, for the cases did not typically evoke the response, 'Now you have told me about these interesting cases, I will reform my usage of the term "knowledge".' The typical response was that it had never been true justified belief that was the crucial factor, but it took the cases to make this obvious, to make explicit what had been implicit in our classificatory practice all along. Also, a theoretical consideration came into play: the Gettier cases are cases of getting something right by a kind of fluke or accident, and it is obviously desirable to have a classification in epistemology for non-flukey success. Those few, noted earlier, who resolutely and unconfusedly insist that the Gettier cases are cases of knowledge are, we argued, right about what counts as knowledge in *their* sense, but, all the same, still need a word for non-flukey success.

For a final example, take the debate over whether a contradiction entails everything. This debate should not be approached by eyeballing some contradiction or other and asking whether one is prepared to say it entails everything. The debate is over whether the relation that plays the distinctive role we give entailment is a role that consistency demands be held to obtain between a contradiction and everything. The central cases for which we use the word 'entails' are important to the debate, but their bearing on the point in dispute turns on whether the right way to *extend* from those cases has the consequence that a contradiction entails everything.

In sum, the business of extracting the cases that count as *K*s from a person's responses to possible cases is an exercise in hypothetico-deduction. We are seeking the hypothesis that best makes sense of their responses taking into account all the evidence.

I am sometimes asked—in a tone that suggests that the question is a major objection—why, if conceptual analysis is concerned to elucidate what governs our classificatory practice, don't I advocate doing serious opinion polls on people's responses to various cases?

My answer is that I do—when it is necessary. Everyone who presents the Gettier cases to a class of students is doing their own bit of fieldwork, and we all know the answer they get in the vast majority of cases. But it is also true that often we know that our own case is typical and so can generalize from it to others. It was surely not a surprise to Gettier that so many people agreed about his cases.

Folk Theory and the Causal–Historical Theory of Reference: A False Opposition

My intuitions about which possible cases to describe as cases of *K*-hood, to describe using the term '*K*', reveal my theory of *K*-hood (remembering, but suppressing in the interests of keeping things simple, that this 'revelation' may be far from straightforward). In as much as my intuitions are shared by the folk, they reveal the folk theory. This will sound like the Lewis–Ramsey–Carnap theory of the reference of theoretical terms.[8] And, accordingly, my defence of conceptual analysis will sound committed to a controversial theory of reference.

This is how Bill Lycan sees the situation. Lycan contrasts two ways you might approach the question of the existence of belief. He says:

I am at pains to advocate a very liberal view. Unlike David Lewis, and unlike Dennett . . . I am entirely willing to give up fairly large chunks of our commonsensical or platitudinous theory of belief or of desire . . . and decide we were just plain wrong about a lot of things, without drawing the inference that we are no longer talking about belief or desire. To put the matter crudely, I incline away from Lewis's Carnapian and/or Rylean cluster theory of the reference of theoretical terms, and towards Putnam's causal-historical theory. As in Putnam's examples of 'water', 'tiger', and so on, I think the ordinary word 'belief' (qua theoretical term of folk psychology) points dimly towards a natural kind that we have not fully grasped and that only mature psychology will reveal. I expect that 'belief' will turn out to refer to some kind of information-bearing inner state of a sentient being . . . but the kind of state it refers to may have only a few of the properties usually attributed to beliefs by common sense.[9]

    [8] David Lewis, 'How to Define Theoretical Terms', *Journal of Philosophy*, 67 (1970): 427–46.
    [9] William G. Lycan, *Judgement and Justification* (Cambridge: Cambridge

I of course hold against Lycan that if we give up too many of the properties common sense associates with belief as represented by the folk theory of belief, we do indeed change the subject, and are no longer talking about belief. The role of the intuitions about possible cases so distinctive of conceptual analysis is precisely to make explicit our implicit folk theory and, in particular, to make explicit which properties are really central to some state's being correctly described as a belief. For surely it *is* possible to change the subject, and how else could one do it other than by abandoning what is most central to defining one's subject? Would a better way of changing the subject be to abandon what is *less* central?

I think that Lycan—and others; I choose Lycan's formulation because of its clarity and directness—misconstrues the relevance to folk theory of what we learnt from Putnam (and Kripke).[10] Putnam built his impressive case concerning the reference of theoretical terms out of intuitions about how to describe possible cases. He told stories about, for famous example, Twin Earth, and invited us to agree with him that what counted as water on Twin Earth was not the stuff on Twin Earth with the famous superficial properties of water—being a clear potable liquid and all that; for short, being watery[11]—but rather the stuff that on Earth made up (most of) the watery samples that we were acquainted with when the term 'water' was introduced. We agreed with Putnam.[12] But we were not under external instruction from some linguistic dictator to agree with him. Our agreement was endogenous. It, there-

---

University Press, 1988), 31–2. Lycan also mentions Stich along with Lewis and Dennett, but I take it from Stephen Stich, 'What is a Theory of Mental Representation?', *Mind*, 101 (1992): 243–61, that he should no longer be included as one of Lycan's targets.

[10] Kripke, *Naming and Necessity*; Putnam, 'The Meaning of "Meaning"'.

[11] Or the watery stuff, as Chalmers puts it, *The Conscious Mind*, 57.

[12] Some of us agreed with him less whole-heartedly than others. See e.g. Frank Jackson, 'A Note on Physicalism and Heat', *Australasian Journal of Philosophy*, 56 (1980): 26–34. I am sympathetic to the view advanced most especially by David Lewis, 'Reduction of Mind', in Samuel Guttenplan, ed., *A Companion to the Philosophy of Mind* (Oxford: Basil Blackwell, 1994), 412–31, see p. 424, that in the mouths and from the pens of the folk it is indeterminate whether it is H_2O or the watery stuff on Twin Earth that counts as water on Twin Earth, and the effect of the stories was to resolve the indeterminacy in the direction of H_2O—at least when we are in 'philosophical' contexts. For simplicity I will suppress this complication in what follows and will suppose, with the majority, that the stories did not resolve an ambiguity but rather made conspicuous a hitherto unremarked feature of our use of the word 'water' and like natural-kind terms.

fore, reflected our folk theory of water. Putnam's theory is built precisely on folk intuitions.

Indeed, and I mention this now because it will be important later, we learn two things from Putnam's story. As has been widely noted, we can think of the Twin Earth story in two different ways, depending on whether we think of Twin Earth as somewhere remote from Earth but in our, the actual, world, or as in another possible world altogether.[13] From the first version, we learn the importance of acquaintance in determining the reference of the word 'water'. The reason the watery XYZ on Twin Earth—a planet located, let's suppose, in Earth's orbit but on the opposite side of the Sun—does not count as water is that it was not XYZ that we were acquainted with when the word 'water' and its cognates in other languages were introduced (and have continued to be acquainted with).[14] From the second version, we learn that the term 'water' is a rigid designator. Even if Twin Earth is simply Earth (or its counterpart) in another possible world, and in that possible world XYZ is both watery and the stuff we—not the Twin Earthians—are acquainted with, it does not count as water. The term 'water' in our mouths and from our pens rigidly denotes whatever *actually* is both watery and is what we are, or certain of our linguistic forebears were, acquainted with.[15] The reference in all worlds is settled by what is watery and the subject of the relevant acquaintance in the actual world. But both our lessons were

---

[13] Though sometimes when the point is noted, it is suggested that it is of no moment which way we think of the Twin Earth parable. If what I say in the text is right, this is a mistake. The discussion in Hilary Putnam's retrospective piece on Twin Earth, 'Is Water Necessarily H$_2$O?', in James Conant, ed., *Realism with a Human Face* (Cambridge, Mass.: Harvard University Press, 1990), 54–79, suggests that he was more concerned with the 'remote place in our world' reading of the parable.

[14] There are nice questions of when historical acquaintance does and does not trump current acquaintance in determining reference, when it is indeterminate which trumps which, and how conversational context affects these matters. But, for our purposes, we can set them to one side. There is also the question of *how* it comes to be that some kind of causal acquaintance is important in determining reference. I favour the view, sometimes known as causal descriptivism (see e.g. Fred Kroon, 'Causal Descriptivism', *Australasian Journal of Philosophy*, 65 (1987): 1–17) that it does so because we use the word 'water' for something that we believe to have, among other properties, the property of being the subject of a certain kind of causal acquaintance.

[15] To put the point in the terms of Martin Davies and Lloyd Humberstone, 'Two Notions of Necessity', *Philosophical Studies*, 38 (1980): 1–30.

lessons about folk theory because they were supported by folk intuitions about possible cases.[16]

As it happens, I do not find very appealing Lycan's view that the
term 'belief' is a term for an informational natural kind whose
identity will be revealed by psychological investigation of (presumably) us exemplars of believers. I think the folk are strongly against

[16] Two cautionary notes about terminology. First, Lycan is clearly writing in
the same tradition as I am, a broadly Quinean (and for that matter Kripkean) one,
I take it, in which were it the case that 'water' was simply an abbreviated definite
description, it would still be true that 'water' *referred*. But there is another, more
Russellian tradition, I take it, according to which most definite descriptions do not
refer at all, and talk of non-rigid reference is a contradiction in terms. See, for example, the remarks in Gareth Evans, 'Reference and Contingency', *Monist*, 62
(1979): 161–89. As far as the discussion here is concerned, I take it that this dispute
is, in Mark Johnston's term, a matter of book-keeping. Incidentally, Evans's remarks in the introduction to *The Varieties of Reference* (Oxford: Clarendon Press,
1982) suggest that he might agree (see esp. pp. 2–3). Secondly, it is sometimes suggested by direct reference theorists that the reference of words in general has nothing to do with the properties we associate with them. But this cannot be true for the
wide sense of 'reference' that I, and I'm taking it Lycan, have in mind. For we use
words to say what things are like—where the tigers and the best beer are, which is
the quickest way home, and so on and so forth—and to say what things are like is
to ascribe properties to them. Perhaps (*perhaps*) for some words, including proper
names, their reference has nothing to do with an associated set of properties. But
this had better not be true for all words on all legitimate notions of reference
thought of as a word–world relation, otherwise we cannot say how things are with
words. And we can and do. Having effectively set to one side the question of
whether the reference of proper names goes by associated properties, I will allow
myself the comment that I am unconvinced by the usual counter-examples—they
all seem to me to be cases where the associated properties (a) vary greatly from person to person, context to context, and are vague, (b) concern causal-information
links especially, or (c) concern properties involving the words themselves, like being
called 'London' by . . ., rather than being examples where there are no associated
properties. To take a recent example, Howard Wettstein, 'Cognitive Significance
without Cognitive Content', in Joseph Almog, John Perry, and Howard Wettstein,
eds., *Themes from Kaplan* (New York: Oxford University Press, 1989), 421–54, says,
p. 439, 'Felipe Alou, I know, was a major-league baseball player. I don't know much
else about him, surely not enough to individuate him in any serious way from many
others, and yet I can use his name to say things about him.' However, 'Felipe Alou'
is a rather unusual name. So Wettstein almost certainly does know something that
individuates him, namely, that he is the only major-league baseball player with that
name. And even if there are a number of players with that name, most likely (a)
only one lies at the end of a causal-information chain with the tokens of the name
that Wettstein has come across at the other, and (b) Wettstein knows this.

All the cases I know where it is intuitively compelling that someone is success-
fully referring when they use a name '*N*' are cases where the person could give a
procedure for identifying the thing referred to if all went well. But then they know
something that individuates the thing in question: it is that which would be identified via its being thus and so if this and that happened.

chauvinism in psychology. Something can be a believer without belonging to the same informational natural kind as we do: being a believer is not like being a tiger. But suppose that he is right, what would show that he is? Surely, just this. When presented with the hypothesis that some creature C belongs to the same informational natural kind as us exemplars of believers, even though, for whatever reason, C does not display the properties characteristic of the exemplars, we find it plausible to say that C has beliefs; conversely, when presented with some possible creature that manifests the properties we associate with the exemplars of belief but belongs to a different informational natural kind, we find it implausible to say that that creature has beliefs. But then what is being revealed by these responses is precisely that the property intuition associates with belief is belonging to the right informational natural kind. So it cannot be right to say, as Lycan does, that a state might be a belief without having the properties we usually associate with belief. *If* intuition delivers the answers it needs to for Lycan's claim to be plausible, the property we folk associate with belief is belonging to the right informational natural kind, and that property is precisely the one that Lycan thinks that all believers have.

I have occasionally come across an extreme view according to which we are supposed to have learnt from Putnam that reference by terms in science is essentially to natural kinds. But surely we *could* have used the 'water' so that it referred to *anything* watery, and it is plausible that nutritionists in fact use a word like 'vitamin' to refer to anything that does a certain nutritional job independently of whether the various substances that do the job form a natural kind. Of course, 'natural kind' is a vague, elastic term. Perhaps the view I am calling 'extreme' should really be recast as the innocuous view that if something is worth referring to with a single word in a science, then it counts as a member of the relevant natural kind in some (pretty relaxed) sense of that term.

The Case for Conceptual Analysis in a Sentence (or Two)

With all this behind us, we can state the rationale for conceptual analysis. Serious metaphysics requires us to address when matters described in one vocabulary are made true by matters described in another. But how could we possibly address this question in the absence of a consideration of when it is right to describe matters in the terms of the various vocabularies? And to do that is to reflect on which possible cases fall under which descriptions. And that in turn is to do conceptual analysis. Only that way do we define our subject—or, rather, only that way do we define our subject as the subject we folk suppose is up for discussion. It is always open to us to stipulate the situations covered by the various descriptive terms, in which case we address subjects of our stipulation rather than the subjects the titles of our books and papers might naturally lead others to expect us to be addressing.

SOME PROPERTIES OF CONCEPTUAL ANALYSIS SO CONCEIVED

It Plays a Modest Role

Conceptual analysis is sometimes given a modest role, and some-times an immodest role. Consider, to illustrate the distinction, a passage from an attack by Peter Geach on four-dimensionalism's treatment of change. He argues that, on the four-dimensionalists' view,

the variation of a poker's temperature with time would simply mean that there were different temperatures at different positions along the poker's time axis. But this, as McTaggart remarked, would no more be a *change* in temperature than a variation of temperature along the poker's length would be. Similarly for other sorts of change.[17]

As this stands, this is a piece of *modest* conceptual analysis. Geach is giving voice to his intuition that different temperatures at differ-ent positions on a time axis does not count as a change in temper-ature—for that you need the very same subject, in some strong sense, to be different temperatures at different times; different tem-poral parts, or whatever, being at different temperatures does not count—and betting that we folk will find his intuition compelling. He is not making any claim, one way or the other, about what the world is like; his claim is simply that if four-dimensionalism is true, it is right to say that nothing changes in the folk sense of change. But, of course, many have taken this kind of consideration to show

[17] P. T. Geach, 'Some Problems about Time', in *Logic Matters* (Oxford: Basil Blackwell, 1972), 302–18, at 304.

that four-dimensionalism *qua* thesis about what our world is like is false. They, in effect, argue as follows:

Pr. 1 Different things (temporal parts or whatever) having different properties is not change. (Conceptual claim illustrated in the case of temperature)

Pr. 2 Things change. (Moorean fact)

Conc. Four-dimensionalism is false. (Claim about the nature of our world)[18]

We now have an example of conceptual analysis in what I call its immodest role. For it is being given a major role in an argument concerning what the world is like.

Or consider the example of rotating, completely homogeneous objects—usually supposed to be disks, spheres, or cylinders—which are symmetrical around the axis of rotation.[19] Our intuitive responses to these examples suggest that we folk distinguish more possibilities concerning motion than the four-dimensionalist treatment of motion can allow. We allow possible differences with respect to motion when how things are at times is exactly the same. Modest conceptual analysis restricts itself to drawing the conclusion that the four-dimensionalist concept of motion may not be the same as the folk concept.[20] Immodest conceptual analysis goes on to draw the conclusion that the four-dimensionalist picture of what the world is like is mistaken.

I think that we should be suspicious of conceptual analysis in its immodest role—it gives intuitions about possibilities too big a

---

[18] Geach offers effectively this argument immediately following the quoted passage, but with an additional support in the form of a 'no change, no time' argument for the second, Moorean premiss.

[19] Discussed in D. M. Armstrong, 'Identity through Time', in Peter van Inwagen, ed., *Time and Cause: Essays Presented to Richard Taylor* (Dordrecht: Reidel, 1980), 67–78; Sydney Shoemaker, 'Identity, Properties, and Causality', in his *Identity, Cause, and Mind* (Cambridge: Cambridge University Press, 1984), 234–60; and Saul Kripke in lectures. I should emphasize that though they discuss essentially the same example, these writers put it to very different uses, and, as I understand them, neither Armstrong nor Shoemaker draws the immodest conclusion I am about to discuss.

[20] I say 'may not' rather than 'is not', because when we include causal dependencies as facts about how things are at times, intuitions about the relevant versions of the spinning disk, sphere, or cylinder are no longer so clear. See e.g. Denis Robinson, 'Matter, Motion and Humean Supervenience', *Australasian Journal of Philosophy*, 67 (1989): 394–409.

place in determining what the world is like.[21] However, the role for conceptual analysis that I am defending in these lectures is the modest role: the role is that of addressing the question of what to say about matters described in one set of terms *given* a story about matters in another set of terms. Conceptual analysis is not being given a role in determining the fundamental nature of our world; it is, rather, being given a central role in determining what to say in less fundamental terms given an account of the world stated in more fundamental terms.

The Sense in Which we Pay Due Homage to Quine's Critique of Analyticity

A defence of conceptual analysis naturally suggests a commitment to a strong version of the analytic–synthetic distinction.[22] But in fact the modest role we are giving conceptual analysis allows us to agree in practice with, while dissenting in theory from, W. V. Quine's famous critique.

There is nothing sacrosanct about folk theory. It has served us well but not so well that it would be irrational to make changes to it in the light of reflection on exactly what it involves, and in the light of one or another empirical discovery about us and our world. Speaking for my part, my pre-analytic conception of free action is one that clashes with determinism. I find compelling Peter van Inwagen's argument that because the past is outside our control, and any action fully determined by something outside our control is not free, determinism is inconsistent with free will.[23] And so do many. Even the most dedicated compatibilists identify it as *the* argument they need to rebut. What compatibilist arguments show, or so it seems to me, is not that free action as understood by the folk is compatible with determinism, but that free action on a conception near enough to the folk's to be regarded as a natural extension of it, and which does the theoretical job we folk give the

---

[21] Thus, my current doubts about the knowledge argument of e.g. Frank Jackson, 'What Mary Didn't Know', *Journal of Philosophy*, 83 (1986): 291–5.

[22] See e.g. Gilbert Harman, 'Doubts about Conceptual Analysis', in John O'Leary Hawthorne and Michaelis Michael, eds., *Philosophy in Mind* (Dordrecht: Kluwer, 1994), 43–8.

[23] Peter van Inwagen, *An Essay on Free Will* (Oxford: Clarendon Press, 1983).

concept of free action in adjudicating questions of moral responsibility and punishment, and in governing our attitudes to the actions of those around us, is compatible with determinism. There is, accordingly, an extent to which the compatibilist is changing the subject, but it is a strictly limited sense. For compatibilists do, it seems to me, show, first, that the folk concept of free action involves a potentially unstable attempt to find a middle way between the random and the determined, second, that the folk conception is nowhere instantiated, and, third, that a compatibilist substitute does all we legitimately require of the concept of free action. It is hard to see how we could better motivate a limited change of subject.

But now what we are doing is very like what Quine calls paraphrasing. As he puts it, 'The objective would not be synonymy, but just approximate fulfilment of likely purposes of the original sentences . . .'.[24] Take a second example. I take it that our folk concept of personal identity is Cartesian in character—in particular, we regard the question of whether *I* will be tortured tomorrow as separable from the question of whether someone with *any* amount of continuity—psychological, bodily, neurophysiological, and so on and so forth—with me today will be tortured tomorrow.[25] But critical reflection of the style initiated most famously by Locke reveals—or so it seems to me and many—that personal identity so conceived is not worth having, and is nowhere instantiated. It is, thus, only sensible to seek a different but 'nearby' conception that does, or does near enough, the job we give personal identity in governing what we care about, our personal relations, our social institutions of reward and punishment, and the like, and which is realized in our world. Certain continuities between how persons are at various times arguably fit the bill, and so we should analyse personal identity in terms of such continuities. Again, what guides us is very like what guides the Quinean who refuses to talk of synonymy, but seeks paraphrases that do the jobs that need doing.

Of course, there remains a fundamental theoretical disagreement about the possibility of there being analytic sentences, the

---

[24] W. V. Quine, *Word and Object* (Cambridge, Mass.: MIT Press, 1960), § 46.
[25] See e.g. Bernard Williams, 'The Self and the Future', *Philosophical Review*, 79 (1970): 161–80. Continuity in these discussions means, of course, causally underwritten continuity.

sentences that could only come false by virtue of meaning change. But anyone who likes the possible-worlds approach to meaning and linguistic representation must, I think, hold that good sense can be made, in one way or another, of the relevant notion of synonymy for words and sentences in a language L. The basic idea behind this approach is to think of their meanings (in the sense relevant to this discussion) as some kind of construction out of the totality of possible situations users of L employ these words and sentences for when seeking to communicate how they take things to be. Quine challenged us to explain the meaning relations required to explicate the notion of analyticity without a too immediate, and so uselessly circular, appeal to analyticity itself.[26] The possible worlds approach is one way of responding to this challenge. It starts from the point that language is a system of representation. It combines this with the point that any system of representation requires a notion of representational content, and the claim that the best approach to representational content is in terms of possible worlds (in the wide sense of 'things' that can be said to accord, or not to accord, with how things are being represented to be). But then the key meaning relations can, somehow or other, be explicated in terms of sets of possibilities.[27] However, the point remains that, in practice, the role I am recommending for conceptual analysis will often be *very* like the role Quine gives the notion of paraphrase.

The Sense in Which Conceptual Analysis Gives A Priori Results

Our account sees conceptual analysis of K-hood as the business of saying when something counts as a K; and we insisted that if we want to have an audience, we had better address the question of when things count as a K, not just for ourselves, but for our audience, the folk, subject to two provisos. First, if our audience should happen to be, say, theoretical physicists, and our subject to be phrased in terms local to theoretical physics, it would be the intuitions and stipulations of this special subset of the folk that would

[26] Most famously in W. V. Quine, 'Two Dogmas of Empiricism,' reprinted in *From a Logical Point of View* (New York: Harper & Row, 1963), 20–46.

[27] See e.g. David Lewis, *Convention* (Cambridge, Mass.: Harvard University Press, 1969).

hold centre stage; and, secondly, as we have lately emphasized, we should be prepared to make sensible adjustments to folk concepts, and this may involve a certain, limited massaging of folk intuitions. Our account sees conceptual analysis as an empirical matter in the following sense. It is an empirical fact that we use a certain term for the kinds of situations and particulars that we do in fact use it for, and the conclusions we come to on the subject are fallible—as Gettier made vivid for us when he showed us that fine conceptual analysts like Ayer and Chisholm got it wrong in the case of the word 'knowledge'. We also noted that conceptual analysis in our sense is of a kind with what cognitive psychologists do when they investigate the young child's concept of *faster than*, and political scientists do when they investigate different voters' concept of *socialist*, and these are, of course, empirical investigations. The question we now face, accordingly, is: In what sense is conceptual analysis concerned with the a priori? For surely *conceptual* analysis must somehow concern the a priori. We know that being fallible and being a priori can co-exist—the results of long numerical additions are well-known examples—but, all the same, the onus is on us to detail the a priori part of the story.

To answer this question, I need to draw a distinction between two fundamentally different senses in which a term can be thought of as applying in various possible situations, or a sentence can be thought of as being true at various possible worlds. The distinction is implicit in Kripke's writings on the necessary a posteriori, and explicit in various subsequent writings on his work by Pavel Tichy, Robert Stalnaker, David Lewis, Martin Davies and Lloyd Humberstone, and, most recently, David Chalmers.[28] I will focus on making the distinction for descriptive terms rather than for sentences, although the extension to the case of sentences will be obvious enough. (And will concern us in the next chapter.)

We can think of the various possible particulars, situations,

---

[28] Kripke, *Naming and Necessity* (Oxford: Basil Blackwell, 1980); Pavel Tichy, 'Kripke on Necessity A Posteriori', *Philosophical Studies*, 43 (1983): 225–41; Robert C. Stalnaker, 'Assertion', in P. Cole, ed., *Syntax and Semantics*, ix (New York: Academic Press, 1978), 315–32; Martin Davies and I. L. Humberstone, 'Two Notions of Necessity', *Philosophical Studies*, 38 (1980): 1–30; David Lewis, 'Index, Context and Content', in Stig Kanger and Sven Öhman, eds., *Philosophy and Grammar* (Dordrecht: Reidel, 1981), 79–100; and David Chalmers, *The Conscious Mind*, 56–65.

events, or whatever to which a term applies in two different ways, depending on whether we are considering what the term applies to under various hypotheses about which world is the actual world, or whether we are considering what the term applies to under various counterfactual hypotheses. In the first case, we are considering, for each world w, what the term applies to in w, given or under the supposition that w is the actual world, our world. We can call this the A-extension of term T in world w— 'A' for actual—and call the function assigning to each world the A-extension of T in that world, the A-intension of T.[29] In the second case, we are considering, for each world w, what T applies to in w given whatever world is in fact the actual world, and so we are, for all worlds except the actual world, considering the extension of T in a counterfactual world. We can call this the C-extension of T in w— 'C' for counterfactual—and call the function assigning to each world the C-extension of T in that world, the C-intension of T.[30] There is no ambiguity about the extension of a term at the actual

[29] It might be asked whether we can make sense of considering, for a *number* of worlds, what a term applies under the supposition that that world is the actual world. Isn't 'actual' the kind of rigid term that necessarily denotes exactly one world? (Richard Holton suggested to me that this is the objection Scott Soames is making in his review of Gareth Evans, *Collected Papers* (Oxford: Clarendon Press, 1985), *Journal of Philosophy*, 86 (1989): 141–56, at 148–9. Soames is discussing Evans's 'Reference and Contingency'.) But consider someone blindfolded and kidnapped who, on hearing their captors saying, 'We are here at last', wonders where 'here' is. Despite the rigidity of the term 'here', their wondering is perfectly sensible. They are wondering where the talking is happening. Likewise, when we consider the A-extension of a term under various hypotheses about which world is the actual world, we are considering the extension of the term under various hypotheses about the world in which we are located (as we can put it if Lewis is right about our being worldbound individuals) or about the kind of world that is actual (to put it more neutrally).

[30] Chalmers, *The Conscious Mind*, calls the A-extension of a term in all possible worlds, its primary intension, and the C-extension of a term in all possible worlds, its secondary intension. Others distinguish horizontal from diagonal senses (and horizontal from diagonal propositions, if they are talking about sentences rather than terms). And still others distinguish information or semantic content from linguistic meaning; for a recent example of the latter, see Fred Adams and Robert Stecker, 'Vacuous Singular Terms', *Mind and Language*, 9 (1994): 387–401— information content is closest to our C-intension, and linguistic content is all but our A-intension. Because of the role acquaintance typically plays in settling the A-extension (but not C-extension) at a world, we need strictly to talk of *centred* worlds in something like W. V. Quine's sense in 'Propositional Objects', in *Ontological Relativity and Other Essays* (New York: Columbia University Press, 1969), 139–60, but I simplify.

world, as the A and C-extension at the actual world must, of course, be the same. For some words, moreover, the A-extension in a world and the C-extension in a world are always the same; that is, their A and C-intensions are the same. An example is the word 'square'. The things in a world that the word 'square' applies to under the hypothesis that that world is the actual world are the very same things that the word 'square' applies to under the hypothesis that that world is a counterfactual world.

However, as we learned from Kripke, this is not true for many words, including natural kind terms like 'water'. 'Water' is a rigid designator for the kind common to the watery exemplars we are, or the appropriate baptizers in our language community were, acquainted with. This is what we grasp when we come to understand the word. This is what we all knew about water before 1750, before we discovered the chemical composition of water. What then does the word 'water' denote in a world where the kind common to the relevant watery exemplars in that world is kind K under the supposition that that world is the actual world? Kind K, of course, be that kind H_2O, XYZ, or whatever. In short, we take Kripke's story about reference fixing, and apply it to each world under the supposition that it is the actual world, to get the A-extension of 'water' in that world. But the answer to what the word 'water' denotes in any world under the hypothesis that that world is a counterfactual world is, of course, H_2O, because the watery stuff in the actual world is H_2O, and 'water' is a rigid designator of whatever it is that is the actual watery stuff. In sum, the A-extension of the term 'water' in a world is the watery stuff of our acquaintance in that world, and the C-extension is H_2O. To avoid possible misunderstanding, I should emphasize that the A-extension of a word at a world may be settled by underlying nature, even when it differs from its C-extension at some worlds. A-extension is not necessarily tied to *superficial* nature. Even beginning chemistry students, whose only way of picking out the acids is by the superficial property of turning litmus paper red, may know that 'acid' applies to something by virtue of its having an underlying nature that plays a specified, significant role in chemical theory that they hope to learn about in future classes. For them, the A-extension of 'acid' at w is what has the *underlying* nature that plays the specified role *in w*, and they know that this extension may include substances that fail to turn litmus paper red. But if 'acid' is indeed a rigid designator, then the C-extension of 'acid' at w is *proton donor* regardless of whether that property plays *in w* a significant role in chemical theory; it plays that role in the actual world (on the Brönsted–Lowry theory), which is what matters for the C-extension.

When a term's A-extension and C-extension differ at some worlds—when it is a two-dimensional term, as we might say in honour of the role of two-dimensional modal logic in making all this explicit—there is a crucial difference between the epistemic status of a term's A-extension and its C-extension. To know a term's C-extension, we need to know something about the actual world. Although we understood the word 'water' before 1750, we did not know its C-extension at a world for any world other than the actual world. The point is not that we did not know the essence of water—we rarely know the essence of the things our words denote (indeed, if Kripke is right about the necessity of origin, we do not know our own essences); the point is that in order to pick out water in a counterfactual world, we need to know something about *relationships* between the counterfactual world and the actual world that we could only know after discovering that in the actual world H_2O plays the watery role. We could be told all there is to know about some counterfactual world w as it is in itself, but until we know something about the actual world, namely, what plays the watery role in it, we would be quite unable to say what was water in w. By contrast, we did know the A-extension of 'water' at every world, for its A-extension does not depend on the nature of the actual world. Ignorance about the actual world does not matter for knowledge about the A-extensions of words.[31] For the A-extension of T at a world w is the extension of T at w *given* w is the actual world, and so does not depend on whether or not w is in fact the actual world. Or, in other words, knowledge of the A-intension of T does not require knowledge of the nature of the actual world. By contrast, in general, knowledge of C-intensions does require knowing the relevant facts about the actual world.

---

[31] Though it does matter for knowledge of the *essences* of A-extensions. We did not know the essence of the A-extension of 'water' in the actual world, for instance, until some time after 1750, but we could identify the A-extension at it and, indeed, at every world. This is not surprising. I do not know my tennis racquet's essence given the necessity of origin, but can identify it.

What we can know independently of knowing what the actual world is like can properly be called a priori. The sense in which conceptual analysis involves the a priori is that it concerns A-extensions at worlds, and so A-intensions, and accordingly concerns something that does, or does not, obtain independently of how things actually are.[32] When we do conceptual analysis of K-hood, we address the question of what it takes to be a K in the sense of when it is right, and when it is wrong, to describe some situation in terms of 'K', and so we make explicit what our subject is when we discuss Ks. The part of this enterprise that addresses the question of what things are K at a world, under the supposition that that world is the actual world, is the a priori part of conceptual analysis, because the answer depends not at all on which world is in fact the actual world (just as the question as to what ought to be done if it is sunny does not depend on whether or not it is sunny). Hostility to conceptual analysis is often characterized as hostility to 'the view that philosophers should spend their time analysing concepts and laying out connections existing in the Platonic realm'.[33] On our conception, the Platonic realm does not come into it; we are simply concerned with making explicit what is, and what is not, covered by some term in our language.

I said earlier that conceptual analysis is the business of articulating how to describe possible cases. It will now be clear that I fudged in the interests of giving the broad picture. There are two different things we might mean by articulating how to describe possible cases. We might mean articulating the A-extensions, or we might mean articulating C-extensions, and it is only the answers to the first which are a priori in the explained sense; that is, in the sense that the answer is independent of which world is the actual world. The answers to the second question are in general not a priori. In the case of the two-dimensional terms and concepts, the C-extension is an a posteriori matter.[34] It depends on the nature of

---

[32] See e.g. Chalmers, *The Conscious Mind*, 62.

[33] Jane Heal, *Fact and Meaning: Quine and Wittgenstein on Philosophy of Language* (Oxford: Basil Blackwell, 1989), 1. She is describing a view she takes to be shared by Quine and Wittgenstein.

[34] Although Kripke does not use the terminology of two-dimensional modal logic, the crucial point is implicit in his writings, or so it seems to me. For he insists that sentences of the form 'K is . . .' where 'K' is a natural-kind term, and the dots are filled with an account of how reference to Ks is fixed are a priori, and the way

the actual world. Thus, to stick with the standard example, although the sentence that gives the A-extension of 'water' at every world, namely, 'Water is the watery stuff of our acquaintance', is a priori, the sentence that gives the C-extension of 'water' at every world, namely, 'Water is H_2O', is a posteriori.

There is a second matter that does not depend on which world is the actual world—namely, whether or not the A-intension of a term is different from the C-intension of the term. For they differ if and only if the extension of the term at a world can be made to vary by varying which world is the actual world. And whether this is, or is not, the case is independent of which world is actual. Hence, whether or not a term is a two-dimensional term is a priori in that the answer to it does not depend on the nature of the actual world. So there are two a priori parts to the conceptual analysis story: the part concerned with the A-intensions of various terms, and the part concerned with whether the A-intensions and C-intensions of various terms differ. For instance, it is a priori that the A-extension of 'water' at any world is the watery stuff of our acquaintance, and also a priori that the C-extension of 'water' at some w differs from the watery stuff of our acquaintance at w.

Quine Revisited

I mentioned our theoretical disagreement with Quine earlier, noting that often in practice it does not matter. We are now, though, in a position to say something directly to the theoretical disagreement.

The Quinean position that denies the possibility of full-blown analyticity in the sense of sentences that are genuinely a priori was seen as radical when it was first propounded. Nowadays it is close to orthodoxy.[35] The idea is that we cannot make a clear distinction between what is a priori and what, for instance, is almost cer-

---

reference to Ks is fixed gives the A-extension of K in every possible world, that is, gives the A-intension. See e.g. the discussion of 'heat' on p. 136 of *Naming and Necessity*. What is unclear, to me anyway, is whether Kripke would regard the distinction between A- and C-extensions as applicable to terms other than natural-kind ones.

[35] At least in America. As Hilary Putnam observes, the situation is different in Britain: 'Pragmatism', *Proceedings of the Aristotelian Society*, 95 (1995): 291–306, at 299.

tainly true or very obviously true—between the encyclopedia and the dictionary, as it is sometimes put. I think, however, that it is insufficiently realized just how radical the Quinean position is.

We use language to tell our community and our later selves how things are. Telling how things are requires representational devices, structures that somehow effect a partition in the possibilities. For we say how things are by saying what is ruled in and what is ruled out. The metaphysics of these possibilities is a controversial matter, as we noted earlier, but anyone who reads a map is in the business of ruling in and ruling out some of the possibilities concerning, say, where the source of the river is, or where the nearest town is.

Now suppose that it is impossible to effect a partition among the possibilities independently of how things actually are. No mental state, no linguistic item, no diagram, no system of semaphore, divides the possibilities, except *relative* to how things actually are. Then we can never say, diagram, depict, semaphore, think, . . . how things are. All we can do is say (depict, think, etc.) how they are *if* . . .. We are always in the position of one who only ever tells you what to do if you have high blood pressure, never what to do *simpliciter*. We can say how things are *conditional* on . . ., but can never make an unconditional claim about how things are. We cannot detach. This is a very radical doctrine. It is not that we cannot say with complete precision how things are. We really cannot say how things are at all.

Thus, the Moorean insists that we can effect partitions in how things are in language, in thought, in pictures . . ., independently of how things actually are; independently, that is, of which world is the actual. But now it follows that whenever we have two thoughts, propositions, sentences, sets of flags, or whatever devices of representation they may be, call them R_1 and R_2, such that the actual-world independent partition effected by R_1 and the actual-world independent partition effected by R_2 is such that the set associated with R_1 is a subset of the set associated with R_2, then 'If R_1 then R_2' is a priori, because it is independent of which world is actual that whenever R_1 is true, R_2 is true.

What then is the difference between, on the one hand, being *very* sure that cats are animals, but regarding it as a posteriori, and, on the other, regarding it as a priori that cats are animals? In the first case you have possibilities to which probability might be moved, that you would describe as ones where cats are not an-imals; in the second you would not describe them that way. So there is a difference in principle. In practice you may not have made the decision about how you will use language that settles whether you'd use 'Cats are not animals' to pick out the possibil-ities to which probability should be moved should some *very* sur-prising discoveries be made, or whether you'd use 'There are some things that would count as cats except that they are not animals'. The nature of the possibility is the same in either case; what is un-settled is how you'd pick it out in language—and the latter may be unsettled simply because the possibility is so exotic there is no point in expending energy in deciding ahead of time which way to jump should the need arise. We can, that is, agree with the point emphasized by Hilary Putnam: in practice it is hard to find *sen-tences* in a natural language that are *determinately* a priori.[36] Our failure to decide in advance how we would jump in fantastical, re-mote cases gives philosophers, with their notorious ability to think up fantastical, remote cases, plenty of scope to come up with a case for which it is undecided whether, as it just might be, 'cat' and 'animal' apply, and so is a case where we can be induced, without going against anything determinate in the meanings of the terms, to apply, say, 'cat' and not apply, say, 'animal'. Thus, the case becomes one where cats are not animals. But the right conclusion is not that 'Cats are animals' was determinately not a priori. It is that 'Cats are animals' is determinately not a priori after the story-telling, but before the story-telling began, it was indeterminate whether or not it was a priori.

Although often we have not decided how to describe some in-credibly unlikely, fantastical happening ahead of time, sometimes we have. We have no trouble understanding stories about fantasti-cally unlikely sequences of coin tosses, about long series of bridge hands consisting of only one suit, or about Davidson's swampman. And, to make sense of these stories, we distinguish between what is *very* confidently believed and what defines that which our very

---

[36] See e.g. Hilary Putnam, 'It Ain't Necessarily So', *Journal of Philosophy*, 59 (1962): 658–71. As many have observed, post-Kripke this paper should be thought of as 'It Ain't A Priori So', and for our purposes the issue about analyticity can be thought of as the issue about the a priori. I am indebted here to discussions with Michael Smith.

confident belief is about—which is not to say that the boundary cannot move with time, or is a sharp one.

The next chapter is concerned with two popular objections to conceptual analysis and, most especially, the distinction between metaphysical and conceptual necessity, and its bearing on our enterprise.

CHAPTER 3

Conceptual Analysis and Metaphysical Necessity

IN the last chapter I addressed the relevance of conceptual analysis to the making-true and necessary determination claims that are part and parcel of serious metaphysics. I explained the general rationale for seeing conceptual analysis as central to answering questions about whether how things are as given in one vocabulary makes true an account given in another vocabulary, in terms of the need, first, to avoid acts of faith, and, secondly, to define or identify one's subject. I went on to explain how intuitions about possibilities—the bread and butter of conceptual analysis—bear on the project of defining or identifying one's subject. I emphasized the modest role I am giving conceptual analysis, the fact that giving folk intuitions a prominent place does not commit one to taking a stand against the causal–historical theory of reference, the fact that conceptual analysis, as I conceived it, could allow Quine and Putnam much of what they wanted, and the sense in which conceptual analysis, although fallible, seeks a priori results.

Identifying the sense in which conceptual analysis seeks a priori results required noting the important distinction between a term's A-extension in any world, and a term's C-extension in any world. It is a term's A-extension in any world, and so its A-intension, that is an a priori matter. This is because a term's A-extension in w is its extension *given* that w is *actual*, and so does not depend on which world is in fact actual. As we noted, in saying this we are saying in different words what Kripke was saying when he said that sentences of the form 'K is . . .', where the ellipsis is filled with what reference fixes to K, are a priori—or so it seems to me.

In this chapter I first address two common objections to the need for conceptual analysis, and then turn to the vexed question of the bearing on our whole enterprise of the distinction between conceptual possibility and necessity, on the one hand, and meta-physical possibility and necessity, on the other. This will place us in a position, towards the end of the chapter, to address the question as to whether physicalists, *qua* holders of a metaphysical view, are committed to the logical thesis of the a priori deducibility of the psychological way things are from the physical way things are.

ON TWO OBJECTIONS TO THE NEED FOR CONCEPTUAL ANALYSIS

The Objection from Theory Reduction in Science

I have said a number of times that conceptual analysis is the key to answering questions about whether matters described in one vocabulary make true an account given in some other vocabulary. The objection from theory reduction is that what are commonly known as smooth reductions in science give us an alternative way of answering making-true questions.[1]

Take the classic example. We have a story about gases told in terms of temperature, volume, and pressure; the account known as the thermodynamic theory of gases. We discover that by identifying gases with collections of widely separated, comparatively small, relatively independently moving molecules, and identifying the properties of temperature, pressure, and volume with the appropriate molecular properties—temperature (in ideal gases) with mean molecular kinetic energy, for famous example—we can derive the laws of the thermodynamic theory of gases from the statistical mechanics of molecular motion, and thereby explain them (and, moreover, explain the exceptions to them). In the spirit of Occam, runs the smooth reduction account, we then identify the properties specified in the language of thermodynamics with the relevant properties specified in the language of molecular mechanics. The whole exercise is described as a smooth reduction because the laws of the reduced theory, the thermodynamic theory of gases,

---

[1] For presentations of the 'smooth reductions' approach as applied to eliminativism about intentional states, see Paul Churchland, 'Folk Psychology and the Explanation of Human Behaviour', *Proceedings of the Aristotelian Society*, supp. vol. 62 (1988): 209–21, and Patricia Churchland, *Neurophilosophy* (Cambridge, Mass.: MIT Press, 1986).

are pretty much preserved in, by virtue of being pretty much iso-morphic with, the corresponding laws in the reducing theory, the molecular or kinetic theory of gases.

The objection to our approach is that when we do this, we dis-cover that the molecular way gases are makes true the thermody-namic account of them without reference to conceptual analysis. The story is one about a posteriori discoveries and ontological par-simony, not about concepts. Generalizing, the idea is that smooth reductions justify identifying the entities and properties of a re-duced theory with entities and properties of a reducing theory, and thereby preserve these entities and properties from elimination by the reducing theory, independently of conceptual issues.

However, although the smooth reduction story does not appeal to conceptual analysis explicitly, it appeals to it implicitly. The dis-coveries that lead to the molecular theory of gases show that mean molecular kinetic energy plays the temperature role, that it plays the 'T' role in the ideal gas laws. The readiness of scientists to move straight from this discovery to the identification of tempera-ture in gases with mean molecular kinetic energy told us what their concept of temperature in gases was. It was the concept of that which plays the temperature role in the thermodynamic theory of gases. Moreover, ontological extravagance was never an option. All the causal work we associate with temperature in gases is, it turns out, done by mean molecular kinetic energy. Thus, to hold that temperature in gases is distinct from, but correlated with, mean molecular kinetic energy, would be to embrace not just an ontologically extravagant option, but the absurd one of holding that temperature in gases does nothing. (It is irrelevant whether or not it is abstractly possible that we have here a case of overdeter-mination. We can be confident that we do not in fact have a case of overdetermination.)

When I say that the concept of temperature in gases is the con-cept of that which plays the temperature role, I mean that the *A*-extension of 'temperature in gases' in every world is that which plays the temperature role in gases in that world. The *C*-extension of 'temperature in gases' is mean molecular kinetic energy, and it is a posteriori that temperature in gases is mean molecular kinetic energy. True, the idea that conceptual analysis is the key to show-ing the identity of temperature in gases with mean kinetic energy goes back to early presentations of the mind–brain identity theory by Jack Smart, David Armstrong, and David Lewis, and in these presentations the claim is that a term like 'temperature' is an abbreviation of a definite description like 'the property that plays the temperature role'.[2] This abbreviated definite description view is essential to the scientific identifications of temperature in gases with mean molecular kinetic energy, of lightning with electrical discharge, and so on, appealed to by Smart and Armstrong especially, being examples of contingent (not just a posteriori) identity statements suitable as models for the claimed contingent identity of mental states with brain states.[3] But the case for identifying temperature in gases with mean molecular kinetic energy goes just as well if we instead view playing the temperature role as a piece of reference-fixing, as an elucidation of the *A*-intension of 'temperature'. For we can view the argument below in two ways:

Pr. 1   Temperature in gases = that which plays the temperature ('*T*') role in gases. (Conceptual claim)

Pr. 2   That which plays the temperature role in gases = mean molecular kinetic energy. (Empirical discovery)

Conc. Temperature in gases = mean molecular kinetic energy. (Transitivity of '=')

We can think in the old way of the first premiss as capturing a fact about the meaning of 'temperature in gases' (on one disambiguation of the meaning of 'meaning'), in which case it is both a priori and necessary. Or we can think in the new way of the premiss as capturing a fact about reference-fixing, and so a fact about the *A*-extension in all worlds, that is, the *A*-intension, of 'temperature in gases', in which case the premiss is a priori and contingent.[4] Either

---

[2] D. M. Armstrong, *A Materialist Theory of the Mind* (London: Routledge & Kegan Paul, 1968), and David Lewis, 'An Argument for the Identity Theory', *Journal of Philosophy*, 63 (1966): 17–25. J. J. C. Smart's appeal to topic neutral reports in 'Sensations and Brain Processes', *Philosophical Review*, 68 (1959): 141–56, played the same role in the overall argument for the theory as the more behaviourally oriented, functional analyses offered by Armstrong and Lewis.

[3] It was, of course, the relevant *statements* of the identity that were being claimed to be contingent.

[4] Although Kripke insists that accounts of reference fixing are not accounts of meaning—see *Naming and Necessity*, 55, for a particularly explicit statement—this seems to be more a stipulation about the meaning of 'meaning' than a substantive thesis in its own right. Moreover, we could follow Davies and Humberstone, 'Two

way, the first premiss is a priori and properly called a conceptual claim, and the identity conclusion follows validly from the premisses.

The moral is that smooth reductions in science are not examples that do not involve conceptual analysis. At most, what is true is that sometimes the conceptual analysis involved, or presupposed, is best seen as an elucidation of the *A*-intensions of certain theoretical terms, rather than of their meaning as traditionally understood.

Stich's Challenge, or the Challenge of Actual Cases

I have argued that we need conceptual analysis to establish making-true and necessary determination claims. Applied to physicalism, this means that physicalists who are not eliminativists about *K*s must do some conceptual analysis in order to show how the physical account of the world could make true accounts framed in terms of *K*s.

Stephen Stich has recently argued that this requirement can be seen to be an absurd one if we consider actual cases.[5] But before we consider his argument, let me note in passing a puzzling feature of Stich's paper. He presents himself as a committed opponent of conceptual analysis, understood as the business of finding necessary and sufficient conditions by the method of possible cases, or as he puts it the 'method of proposing definitions and hunting for intuitive counterexamples'.[6] He says, for instance, that '*No* commonsense concept that has been studied has turned out to be analysable into a set of necessary and sufficient conditions'.[7] At the same time, he praises the work of Eleanor Rosch as offering an interesting alternative to the traditional, and in his view misguided,

---

Notions of Necessity', and say that the meaning of 'temperature in gases' is 'that which *actually* plays the temperature role', where the 'actually' fixes the reference in counterfactual worlds to that which plays the temperature role in the actual world.

[5] Stich, 'What is a Theory of Mental Representation?'. Similar sentiments are expressed in Michael Tye, 'Naturalism and the Mental', *Mind*, 101 (1992): 421–41, and Terence Horgan, 'From Supervenience to Superdupervenience: Meeting the Demands of a Material World', *Mind*, 102 (1993): 555–86.

[6] Stich, 'What is a Theory of Mental Representation?', 250.

[7] Ibid.

hunt for necessary and sufficient conditions. Here is the crucial passage.

On the Roschian view, the mental structures that underlie people's judgments when they classify items into categories do not exploit tacitly known necessary and sufficient conditions for category membership . . . Exactly what they do use is an issue that has motivated a great deal of empirical research during the last fifteen years . . . Early on Rosch proposed that categorization depends on *prototypes*, which may be thought of as idealized descriptions of the most typical or characteristic members of the category. The prototype for *bird*, for example, might include such features as flying, having feathers, singing, and a variety of others. In determining whether a particular instance falls within the category, subjects assess the *similarity* between the prototype and the instance being categorized. However, features specified in the prototype are not even close to being necessary and sufficient conditions for membership. So, an animal can lack one or many of the features of the prototypical bird, and still be classified as a bird. Emus are classified as birds although they neither fly nor sing.[8]

The puzzle is that Roschian view he describes as opposed to the search for necessary and sufficient conditions is itself a view about the necessary and sufficient conditions for being a bird: as he himself describes it, the view is that being sufficiently similar to the relevant prototype is necessary and sufficient for being a bird. Moreover, Stich supports the view by pointing out how it fares on the method of cases, for he notes that the view correctly classifies an emu as a bird.

My guess is that he thinks that Rosch's work is not an example of conceptual analysis because it involves empirical research into what guides people in their classificatory practices (this seems to be what influences Tye, who also classifies Rosch's work as inimical to conceptual analysis) but, as we noted in the previous chapter, that is to misunderstand the sense in which conceptual analysis is a priori.[9]

---

[8] Ibid. 249.

[9] George Lakoff, *Women, Fire, and Dangerous Things* (Chicago, Ill.: University of Chicago Press, 1987), also sees Rosch's work as inimical to the search for necessary and sufficient conditions, but here what seems to be at work is a special reading of necessary and sufficient conditions that rules out cluster accounts and is tied to some version of the language of thought. We return to these issues in the discussion of paradigm-based accounts of the use of general terms.

Be all this as it may, what is the challenge of actual cases? I will focus on one example Stich gives (similar points apply to the others). He points out that we cannot, as of now, give an analysis of grooming behaviour in animals in physical terms, and probably never will be able to, and yet it would be absurd to infer from this that we should, as good naturalists cum physicalists, start to doubt whether there is any such phenomenon as animals' grooming each other and themselves.

Stich is right that we cannot write down necessary and sufficient conditions for an animal displaying grooming behaviour in austerely physical terms, but he has misunderstood what we conceptual analysts have in mind when we say that making-true stories need conceptual analysis. What we require from physicalists who accept the existence of grooming behaviour is enough by way of conceptual analysis to make it plausible that the purely physical account of our world makes true the grooming-behaviour account of our world; and to do that it is *not* required to give necessary and sufficient conditions in physical terms for grooming behaviour.

We can make the crucial point with a simple example of the kind mentioned in Chapter 1. Consider the sentence

(1) The average size of houses in 1990 is under 1,000 square metres.

We know that (1) is true. Our understanding of the word 'average' tells us something about what makes (1) true in terms of the way individual houses are. We know that there is some huge, true sentence in some idealized, enlarged form of English with, for instance, a name for every house, that gives the size of every house and how many houses there are, from which (1) follows. But we cannot give this sentence in practice, although possibly we could in principle if enough funding were provided. Moreover, the sentence that gives the necessary as well as sufficient condition for (1) in terms of sentences about individual houses is an infinite disjunction of long conjunctions, giving all the possible ways individual houses might be with respect to size and total number in 1990, that keeps their average size under 1,000 square metres; and that could not be given no matter how much funding was available. Nevertheless, our grasp of the concept of an average in the sense of what we use the word 'average' for, tells us that (1) is made true by the size and number of houses that exist in 1990, and that some complex, very long, true sentence in an idealized extension of English concerning which individual houses there are and their sizes in 1990 entails (indeed, a priori entails) (1).

What we conceptual analysts are demanding of physicalists is that they do something similar to what we should all agree is possible in the case of our little example. Physicalists need to do enough by way of conceptual analysis of grooming behaviour—or belief, or pain, or inflation, or whatever[10]—to make it plausible that the huge, true sentence about the physical way the world is entails that there are cases of grooming behaviour—or belief, or pain, or inflation, or whatever.

This is not the place to decide whether they can do the needed job. I am not seeking to defend physicalism here. But it is important that it is far from obvious that physicalists cannot do the job, or at least not so obvious that it shows the demand for conceptual analysis from physicalists, and serious metaphysicians in general, is an unreasonable one. Analytical functionalism, for example, is an interesting and widely supported account of how it could be that the physical way things are makes true the psychological account of how they are.[11] It comes in two stages. One stage—the most discussed—is an analysis of psychological sentences as sentences about the functional roles of states of subjects. The claim is that it is a priori that belief is a state that tends to fit the facts and that guides us when we seek to realize what we desire, and a priori that desire is a state that tends to get the facts to fit it given what we believe. The analogy is with the sense in which it is a priori that a thermostat is a temperature-regulating device—that's what we use the word 'thermostat' for. And this story about belief and desire, suitably elaborated of course, amounts to a functional account of them. The other stage is about how certain physical facts entail that the appropriate functional-cum-causal states obtain. Again, the story is offered as a conceptual truth. The idea is that a proper understanding of the concept of a functional fact shows

[10] Or of attack behaviour, or of /p/—other examples Stich mentions.

[11] For some defences of one or another variety of analytical functionalism, see Sydney Shoemaker, *Identity, Cause, and Mind* (Cambridge: Cambridge University Press, 1984); David Lewis, 'Psychophysical and Theoretical Identifications', *Australasian Journal of Philosophy*, 50 (1972): 249–58; and Armstrong, *A Materialist Theory of the Mind*.

that functional nature is entailed by the relevant physical facts, including, of course, physical laws.

What, then, of Stich's example of grooming behaviour? On the understanding of the conceptual analysis requirement just given, it surely makes good sense, independently of where you stand on the question of physicalism, that a defence of the existence of grooming behaviour requires conceptual analysis. If Jones explains that by grooming behaviour, she means behaviour likely to solve Goldbach's conjecture, surely the right thing to say is that on *this* understanding of grooming behaviour, non-human animals never display it, although maybe the occasional human animal does. If Smith explains to you that by grooming behaviour he means any behaviour involving contact between limb and body, surely the right thing to say is that on *this* understanding of grooming behaviour, non-human animals most certainly display grooming behaviour. That is to say, the reasonableness of believing in the existence of grooming behaviour is not independent of what we understand by it. What counts, and what does not count, as grooming behaviour is crucial. So when we address the question of the existence of grooming behaviour on the folk understanding, or perhaps the biologically informed folk understanding—presumably the question we were interested in all along—the answer is not independent of what the folk count as grooming behaviour; it is not, therefore, independent of the right way to analyse grooming behaviour. Of course it may not be easy to come up with the right analysis. But the crucial point here, and generally, is that our classifications of things into categories—grooming behaviour, belief, pain, and so on and so forth—is not done at random and is not a miracle. There are patterns underlying our conceptual competence. They are often hard to find—we still do not know in full detail the rules that capture the patterns underlying our classification of sentences into the grammatical and the ungrammatical, or of inferential behaviour into the rational and the irrational—but they must be there to be found. We do not classify sentences as grammatical, or inferential behaviour as rational, by magic or at random!

When I say that the commonalities are there to be found, I do not simply mean that there is some scientific explanation for our classificatory practices—that goes without saying. I mean that typically we know something useful and non-grue-like, and are giving voice to this knowledge when we classify happenings as examples of grooming behaviour, pain, rational inference, and so on.[12] For only then can we explain the manifestly useful information we give about what the world is like to each other and to our later selves, through diary entries and notes on fridges, when we use words like 'pain', 'grooming behaviour', 'electricity bill', 'belief', 'rational', and so on.

When I insist that the relevant knowledge is available to us, although often hard to make explicit, I am not denying the familiar point that our classificatory abilities often rest on our ability to respond to a property without knowing which property we are responding to. It is said, and let's suppose that it is true, that chicken sexers do not know what triggers in them the responses 'It's female' and 'It's male' when they look at newborn chicks.[13] But, of course, the chicken sexers know something *about* the properties that are doing the triggering. They know that they are regularly correlated with an ability in one case, and an inability in the other, to lay eggs in the future. This is the useful information which we get—and poultry farmers pay for—from chicken sexers.

Howard Wettstein distinguishes 'definition-based' from 'paradigm-based' stories about the application of general terms. On the paradigm-based story, one is 'exposed to a certain number of cases, and . . . perhaps corrected on a number of occasions on the application of the term, one [then] gets the feel for what is to count as a genuine application of the term, somewhat like the way one gets the feel for how to serve in tennis'.[14] Wettstein appears to be tempted by the idea that the paradigm-based story applies universally. This seems as a matter of empirical fact false. Surely we learn *some* terms by being given a necessary and sufficient condition in a language we understand. An example is the term 'sibling'. Most of us learnt this term by being told in so many words that a sibling is a brother or sister. However, often the paradigm-based story

---

[12] Though, for terms for with distinct A- and C-intensions, the scientific story will sometimes be the one that tells us the term's C-extension at a world. Also, although we are giving voice to what we folk know, what we know may not be something we can, as of now, give in words. See the discussion of the uncodifiability of rationality below.

[13] A similar claim is sometimes made about lion tamers' ability to tell that a lion is dangerous, and the common ability to say that some arrangement—of flowers, furniture, opposing troops, . . . — has changed even when the respect in which it has changed is unknown.

[14] Wettstein, 'Cognitive Significance without Cognitive Content', 435 n. 28.

applies, but when it does there is, nevertheless, a known commonality to the things that fall under a term '*K*'. At the very least, we know that they are all cases that have a commonality that training has led us to tag '*K*', though typically we know a great deal more than this. When we use the word 'cat', part of what we know is that the creatures we tag 'cat' present a gestalt that we cannot break down exhaustively into its components, but which prompts the word 'cat' in our mouths. But we also know that they are the offspring of cats, are furry, are typically smaller than dogs, and so on and so forth.[15]

Similarly, Gareth Evans in a discussion of discriminating knowledge says: '*Either* the subject is in possession of a formula or criterion for determining whether a given object is *a*—an employment of this formula or criterion would manifest what others have known as "descriptive identification"; or else he possesses, in Dummett's phrase, a *mere* "propensity for recognition".'[16] There is an important distinction here, but it is not happily called that between descriptive identification and something which is not descriptive identification, or so it seems to me; for being disposed to be recognized by a subject as a such-and-such is a descriptive property of something that can and does serve to pick it out from other things. The important distinction is between the kinds of properties that do the picking-out job. Sometimes they are properties that do not involve essentially a relation to a subject, and sometimes, as when they concern dispositions of subjects, they do. Again, it is sometimes said that you can identify things in memory—a certain confrontation with a dog in one's childhood, as it might be—without knowing any property unique to that confrontation. You might, it is argued, have had many such confrontations in your childhood and know nothing that singles out the incident that you recall, yet surely you can have a thought

---

[15] What may have made this point opaque is (a) the correct observation that the C-extension at a world of 'cat' is not given by the list sketched above—but we can, and here should, think in terms of A-extensions, and (b) the suspicion that the story is circular—but we could write out a Ramsey sentence for 'cat', and it is not circular to *mention* 'cat'. On Ramsey sentences, see the discussion in the last two chapters on ethics.

[16] Evans, *The Varieties of Reference*, 93, my emphasis. The reference to Michael Dummett is to *Frege: Philosophy of Language* (London: Duckworth, 1973), 488.

about it and correctly refer to it as the confrontation that you are right now thinking about. But in such a case you do know something that singles the incident out: it is the one that has an information-preserving causal link to your current memory. The important distinction is not between thought about particular things mediated by identifying properties, and thought about particular things not so mediated, but between cases where the mediation is done via relations between the thought in question, or more generally the thinker or subject in question, and what is thought about, as opposed to cases where the thinker knows individuating properties of the object that are not relations between it and thought or thinker.

Again, it is sometimes said that rationality is *uncodifiable*.[17] What is certainly true is that we cannot, as of now, write down in a natural language necessary and sufficient conditions for being rational. (Though we can say something useful and to the point— whatever the defects of the inductive logic sections of textbooks and extant discussions of experimental design, they are very far from useless.) What would be incredible, in my view, would be if there were no story to be told constructible from our folk-classificatory practice: we are finite beings; we do not work by magic; we give useful information to each other by means of the word 'rational'.[18] There must, therefore, be a story to be told (extracted). And when it is told (extracted), rationality will have been codified.

CONCEPTUAL NECESSITY AND METAPHYSICAL NECESSITY[19]

It is time—some will say, more than time—to address an important objection, and to answer an important question. Both arise

---

[17] See e.g. William Child, 'Anomalism, Uncodifiability, and Psychophysical Relations', *Philosophical Review*, 102 (1993): 215–45.

[18] If some forms of non-cognitivism are true, the information may be about attitudes taken rather than about how things are taken to be, but the point stands either way.

[19] I have discussed this issue with more people than I can possibly list but must mention David Braddon-Mitchell, Richard Holton, Lloyd Humberstone, and David Lewis.

from the now famous distinction between metaphysical and conceptual necessity.

The *objection* is that the distinction between metaphysical and conceptual necessity, and the correlative distinction between metaphysical and conceptual possibility, means that we need to rethink completely the global supervenience thesis from which I derived the entry by entailment thesis and, in turn, physicalism's commitment to the physical nature of the world making true the psychological account of the world. We need to ask from the beginning which kinds of possibility—conceptual or metaphysical—we are quantifying over.

The *question* is the relationship between what we are calling an entailment or necessary determination or fixing thesis, and the issue of a priori deducibility. Our case for physicalism's commitment to the entailment of the psychological by the physical rests on showing that physicalism is committed to every possible world with a certain physical character having a certain psychological character. But, it will be said, although every possible world with a certain H_2O character has a certain water character, we cannot a priori deduce water character from H_2O character, because the necessary identity of water with H_2O is a posteriori. The identity is a metaphysical necessity, not a conceptual one. We have, therefore, an important question to address: Should the necessary passage from the physical account of the world to the psychological one that physicalists are committed to if we are right, be placed in the a posteriori or the a priori basket? In other words: Is physicalism committed to an a priori deducibility thesis in addition to an entailment one in the sense we have been giving to entailment? Or, as it is commonly put: Is physicalism committed to conceptual entailments from the physical to the psychological? My answer will be yes.[20] But I need to address the issues raised by the objection first.

Why the Phenomenon of the Necessary A Posteriori does not Require Acknowledging Additional Kinds of Necessity and Possibility

There are two quite different ways of looking at the distinction between necessary a posteriori sentences like 'Water = H_2O', and ne-

---

[20] For defences of the answer no, see Child, 'Anomalism, Uncodifiability, and

cessary a priori ones like '$H_2O = H_2O$' and 'Water = water'.[21] You might say that the latter are analytically or conceptually or logically (in some wide sense not tied to provability in a formal system) necessary, whereas the former are metaphysically necessary, meaning by the terminology that we are dealing with two senses of 'necessary' in somewhat the way that we are when we contrast logical necessity with nomic necessity.[22] On this approach, the reason the necessity of water's being H_2O is not available a priori is that though what is conceptually possible and impossible is available in principle to reason alone given sufficient grasp of the relevant concepts and logical acumen, what is metaphysically possible and impossible is not so available. Knowledge of the metaphysically necessary and possible is, in general, a posteriori. Similarly, it is often suggested that essential properties show that we need to make a distinction in kinds of necessity between metaphysical and conceptual necessity.

I think, as against this view, that it is a mistake to hold that the necessity possessed by 'Water = H_2O' is different from that possessed by 'Water = water', or, indeed, '$2 + 2 = 4$'. Just as Quine insists that numbers and tables exist in the very same sense, and that the difference between numbers existing and tables existing is a difference between numbers and tables, I think that we should insist that water's being H_2O and water's being water are necessary in the very same sense. The difference lies, not in the kind of

Psychophysical Relations', and Michael Lockwood, *Mind, Brain and the Quantum* (Oxford: Basil Blackwell, 1989). Lockwood uses the term 'physicalism' for what is effectively the a priori deducibility thesis, but holds that the metaphysical thesis that *we* are using 'physicalism' for is not committed to the a priori deducibility thesis. Child's argument turns on the claim about the uncodifiability of rationality we discussed above.

[21] Necessary, modulo worlds where there is no water, that is to say. We will later switch to examples like 'If H_2O covers most of the Earth, then water covers most of the Earth' and 'All water is H_2O', where the proviso is not needed.

[22] See e.g. Peter Forrest, 'Universals and Universalisability', *Australasian Journal of Philosophy*, 70 (1992), 93–8, and, for an especially explicit discussion, Lockwood, *Mind, Brain and the Quantum*, 21–3. However, Lockwood's remarks on p. 22 about the unmysterious nature of metaphysical necessity suggest some sympathy with the two-dimensional approach I discuss below, an approach I see as opposed to the two senses view. See also A. C. Grayling, *An Introduction to Philosophical Logic* (Brighton: Harvester Press, 1982), ch. 3. For a recent paper in the philosophy of mind in which the two senses view plays a prominent role, see Stephen Yablo, 'Mental Causation', *Philosophical Review*, 101 (1992): 245–80, esp. 251–7.

necessity possessed, but rather where the labels 'a priori' and 'a posteriori' suggest it lies: in our epistemic access to the necessity they share. As far as I know, Kripke does not address the two senses question directly, but it is worth noting that he says that 'statements representing scientific discoveries about what this stuff *is* . . . are . . . necessary truths in the strictest possible sense', and that they are necessary 'in the highest degree—whatever that means', which suggest that he does not hold a two kinds of necessity view.[23]

I have two reasons for holding that there is only one sense of necessity and possibility in play here. The first is Occamist. We should not multiply senses of necessity beyond necessity. The phenomena of the necessary a posteriori, and of essential properties, can be explained in terms of one unitary notion of a set of possible worlds. The phenomena do not call for a multiplication of senses of possibility and necessity, and in particular for a distinction among the possible worlds between the metaphysically possible ones and the conceptually possible ones.

The Occamist Reason

Take essential properties first. What convinces us that there are essential properties is the intuitive appeal of the claim that, as we go from one possible world to another, there are certain changes that require us to say that we have a different thing rather than the same thing with different properties in the two worlds. A difference in origin, for instance, is said to require us to say that we have two different tables rather than the very same table but with a changed origin. But, in explicating this, we do not appeal to a different sort of necessity. The possible worlds that figure in the story that articulates how a property can be an essential property of x, namely, by being possessed by x in every possible world in which x appears, are to be thought of in the same way—whatever precisely that is—as those that figure in the story about the necessity of '$2 + 2 = 4$'. It is, for instance, supposed to be a priori accessible that a table's identity cannot survive a change in origin as we go from one possible world to another.

---

[23] Kripke, *Naming and Necessity*, 125 and 99, respectively.

The phenomenon of the necessary a posteriori calls for more discussion. We need, it seems to me, to have before us from the beginning two central facts. First, it is sentences, or if you like statements or stories or accounts in the sense of assertoric sentences in some possible language, that are necessary a posteriori.[24] Secondly, the puzzle about the necessary a posteriori is not how a sentence can be necessary and yet it takes empirical work to find this out. Russians utter plenty of sentences which are necessarily true, and yet it takes many of us a lot of empirical work to discover the fact. The puzzle is how a sentence can be necessarily true and understood by someone, and yet the fact of its necessity be obscure to that person. And the reason this is a puzzle is because of the way we use sentences to tell people how things are—a matter we adverted to briefly in Chapter 2 when discussing the a priori.

Consider what happens when I utter the sentence, 'There is a land-mine two metres away.' I tell you something about how things are, and to do that is precisely to tell you which of the various possibilities concerning how things are is actual. My success in conveying this urgent bit of information depends on two things: your understanding the sentence, and your taking the sentence to be true. We have here a folk theory that ties together understanding, truth, and information about possibilities; and the obvious way to articulate this folk theory is to identify, or at least essentially connect, understanding a sentence with knowing the conditions under which it is true; that is, knowing the possible worlds in which it is true and the possible worlds in which it is false; that is, knowing the proposition it expresses on *one* use of the term 'proposition'. This kind of theory in its philosophically sophisticated articulations is best known through the work of David Lewis and Robert Stalnaker.[25] But it would, I think, be wrong to regard the folk theory as being as controversial as these articulations. The folk theory is, it seems to me, a commonplace. The sports section

---

[24] And, in the Preface to *Naming and Necessity*, 20–1, Kripke insists that his concern is with sentences, not propositions.

[25] Lewis, *On the Plurality of Worlds*, and Robert Stalnaker, *Inquiry* (Cambridge, Mass.: MIT Press, 1984). There is notoriously a problem about what to say concerning mathematical sentences within the possible-worlds framework, but our concern is with sentences about relatively mundane items like water and land-mines, and, later, with entailments between sentences putatively representing the way things are as a matter of empirical fact.

of any newspaper is full of speculations about possible outcomes, conveyed by sentences that discriminate among the outcomes in a way we grasp because we understand the sentences. Again, we find our way around buildings by reading or hearing sentences that we understand like 'The seminar room is around the corner on the left'. There are many different places the seminar room might be located, but after seeing or hearing the sentence, and by virtue of understanding it and trusting the person who produces it, we know which of the possibilities is actual. Again, it is no news to the folk that one of the annoying things about not understanding the language of a foreign country is one's inability to use the sentences the locals make available to find one's way around. But now it seems that understanding a necessarily true sentence should, at least in principle, be enough to reveal its necessary status. For understanding it would require knowing the conditions under which it is true, and how could you know them—really know them—and yet fail to notice that they hold universally? The puzzle is particularly pressing when, as in the cases we are concerned with, the sentences are relatively simple ones concerning accessible, contingent features of our world. They are not highly complex ones that we might expect to present comprehension and processing problems.

I think—unoriginally—that the way out of our puzzle is to allow that we understand some sentences without knowing the conditions under which they are true, in *one* sense of the conditions under which they are true, though, as we will note later, we must know the conditions under which they are true in *another* sense of the conditions under which they are true.[26]

Here is an illustrative example, familiar from discussions of

---

[26] I take it that the account which follows is a sketch of the approach naturally suggested by the two-dimensional modal logic treatment of the necessary a posteriori, as in, for instance, Stalnaker, 'Assertion'; Davies and Humberstone, 'Two Notions of Necessity'; David Kaplan, 'Demonstratives', in Joseph Almog, John Perry, and Howard Wettstein, eds., *Themes from Kaplan* (New York: Oxford University Press, 1989), 481–564; Tichy, 'Kripke on Necessity A Posteriori'; Frank Vlach, '"Now" and "Then": A Formal Study in the Logic of Tense and Anaphora' (Ph.D. dissertation, University of California at Los Angeles, 1973); and Lewis, 'Index, Context and Content'. They should not be held responsible for my way of putting matters. What immediately follows in the text can be put in Stalnaker's terminology by saying that understanding requires knowing the propositional concept associated with a sentence, though not necessarily the proposition expressed, and in Kaplan's by saying that understanding requires knowing character but not necessarily content.

two-dimensional modal logic, of understanding a sentence without knowing its truth-conditions in one sense.[27] Suppose I hear someone say 'He has a beard'. I will understand what is being said without necessarily knowing the conditions under which what is said is true, because I may not know who is being spoken of. That is, I may not know which proposition is being expressed. If I am the person being spoken of, the proposition being expressed is that Jackson has a beard; if Jones is the person being spoken of, the proposition being expressed is that Jones has a beard; and so on. Hence, if I don't know whether it is Jackson, Jones, or someone else altogether, I don't know which proposition is being expressed in the sense of not knowing the conditions under which what is said is true. But obviously I do understand the sentence. I understand the sentence because I know how to move from the appropriate contextual information, the information which in this case determines who is being spoken of, to the proposition expressed.

A similar point can be made about 'water' sentences. The propositions expressed by, in the sense of the truth-conditions of, our 'water' sentences depend on how things are in the actual world—in particular, on whether the watery stuff of our acquaintance is H_2O. This means that those who do not know this fact do not know the proposition expressed by, for example, 'Water covers most of the earth'. They could know all there is to know about some counterfactual world without knowing whether the sentence is true in that world—whether that world is a condition under which the sentence is true—through their ignorance about the actual world. Because they do not know which stuff is the watery stuff of our acquaintance in the actual world, they do not know which stuff in the counterfactual world is the watery stuff of our acquaintance in the actual world, and that they need to know to evaluate the sentence in the counterfactual world.[28] Nevertheless, they understand 'water' sentences. It follows that understanding 'Water covers most of the Earth' does not require knowing the conditions under which it is true, that is, the proposition it expresses. Rather it requires knowing how the proposition expressed depends on context of utterance—in this case, how it depends on which

---

[27] The example is a variant on one discussed by Stalnaker, 'Assertion'.

[28] The point here is, of course, essentially the same as the point made about C-extensions in Chapter 2.

stuff in the world of utterance is the watery stuff of our acquaintance in it.

The explanation of the necessary a posteriori is now straightforward. Our question is: How can you understand a necessarily true sentence and yet need a posteriori information to tell you that it is necessary? The answer is because understanding does not require knowing the proposition expressed, and yet it is the nature of the proposition expressed that determines that the sentence is necessary. And the important point for us is that this story about the necessary a posteriori does not require acknowledging two sorts of necessity. The story was all in terms of the one set of possible worlds.

An Unexpected Ally

I know from discussion that many insist that I have completely failed to learn the Twin Earth lesson. I reduce important discoveries about necessity, namely, that it should be sharply divorced from a priority, and that conceptual necessity is quite distinct from metaphysical necessity, to a linguistic phenomenon! So let me cite a piece of evidence from the 'discoverer' of Twin Earth. Hilary Putnam's recent reflections on Twin Earth include the following passage:

When terms are used rigidly, logical possibility becomes dependent upon empirical facts.[29]

At first reading, this is a surprising remark. Surely, a fact about English usage—which terms are rigid and which are not—is not relevant to the acceptability of the principle that something is possible if and only if it is necessary that it is possible? The way to make sense of it, I submit, is as a claim about the *sentences* in which the rigidly used terms appear. But it is hardly news, and anyway not something that needs support from Twin Earth parables, that the modal status of a sentence depends on facts about word usage. It follows from the fact that words and sentences might have had different meanings from those they in fact have. What is interesting, and what it did take Twin Earth considerations to

[29] Putnam, 'Is Water Necessarily H_2O?', 62.

show,[30] is that consistent with fixing what is required for understanding the sentence 'Water = H_2O', we can change its modal status (that is, change the modal status of the proposition it expresses) by changing empirical facts. We can thus make good sense of Putnam's claim by reading it in the style recommended by two-dimensional modal logic.

The 'Other Proposition' Way of Saying What I Have Just Said [31]

I said we can understand certain sentences, 'water' sentences for example, by knowing how the proposition expressed depends on context, and so do not need to know the sentences' truth-conditions. But to know how the proposition expressed depends on context *is* to know truth-conditions in *another* sense of a sentence's truth-conditions. For example, the knowledge required to understand 'Water covers most of the Earth' can be given in the following array:

If H_2O is the watery stuff we are actually acquainted with, then 'Water covers most of the Earth' expresses a proposition that is true iff H_2O covers most of the Earth.

If XYZ is the watery stuff we are actually acquainted with, then 'Water covers most of the Earth' expresses a proposition that is true iff XYZ covers most of the Earth.

and, generalizing,

If . . . is the watery stuff we are actually acquainted with, then 'Water covers most of the Earth' expresses a proposition that is true iff . . . covers most of the Earth.

Although for each distinct, context-giving antecedent concerned with the relevant facts about how things actually are, a distinct proposition is expressed by the sentence, simple inspection of the array shows that the sentence is true if and only if most of the Earth is covered by the watery stuff of our acquaintance. So, in that sense, the understanding producer of the sentence does know

[30] Twin Earth considerations in their 'other possible world' form, not their 'remote place in the actual world' form.
[31] I am much indebted to David Lewis, Pavel Tichy, and David Chalmers here.

when the sentence is true. Accordingly, we could say, following Tichy, Chalmers, Lewis, and Stalnaker among others, that there are *two* propositions connected with a sentence like 'Water covers most of the Earth'. The one we have been calling the proposition expressed is the set of worlds at which the sentence is true given which world is in fact the actual world; the other is the set of worlds satisfying the following condition: given that w is the actual world, then the sentence is true at w. In this second case, we are considering, for each world w, the truth value of S in w under the supposition that w is the actual world, our world. We can call this set of truth-conditions the A-proposition expressed by S—'A' for actual. In the case of the first proposition, however, we are considering, for each world w, the truth value of S, given whatever world is in fact the actual world, and so we are considering, for all worlds except the actual world, the truth-value of S in a counterfactual world. We can call this set of truth-conditions, the C-proposition expressed by T—'C' for counterfactual. Obviously, the A-proposition is an extension to sentences of the A-intension of terms, and the C-proposition is an extension to sentences of the C-intension of terms, that we talked about in the previous chapter. It is, I take it, the C-proposition that is normally meant by unadorned uses of the phrase 'proposition expressed by a sentence' *when* 'proposition' is meant in its set-of-truth-conditions sense.[32]

It is, as Stalnaker, Tichy, and Chalmers emphasize, the A-proposition expressed by a sentence that is often best for capturing what someone believes when they use the sentence, and for capturing the information they seek to convey by uttering a sentence. Thus, children who have not yet had the chemistry lesson in which they are told that water is H_2O, but who understand the sentence 'Water covers most of the Earth', will use the sentence to express their opinion that most of the Earth is covered by the watery stuff of our acquaintance. And, in general, it is the A-proposition we know in virtue of understanding a sentence.

---

[32] As opposed, for instance, to the sense in which propositions are thought of as individuated by the concepts that in some sense make them up. See e.g. Christopher Peacocke, *A Study of Concepts* (Cambridge, Mass.: MIT Press, 1992). For a recent example of the use of 'proposition' to mean what we are calling the C-intension (proposition) and *not* the A-intension (proposition), see Adams and Stecker, 'Vacuous Singular Terms'.

Thus, we have two superficially different but essentially identical accounts of the necessary a posteriori. One says a sentence like 'Water = H_2O' gets to be necessary a posteriori because the proposition it expresses is necessary, but which proposition this is need not be known in order to understand the sentence, and is an a posteriori matter depending on the nature of the actual world. Little wonder then that it takes empirical work and not just understanding, to see that the proposition expressed and, thereby, the sentence, is necessary. The other says that there are two propositions connected with a sentence like 'Water = H_2O', and the sentence counts as necessary if the C-proposition is necessary, but, as understanding the sentence only requires knowing the A-proposition, little wonder that understanding alone is not enough to see that the sentence is necessary. The important point for us is that both stories can be told in terms of one set of possible worlds.

The Second Reason for Denying the 'Two Senses' View

My second reason for holding that there is one sense of necessity and possibility, that the labels 'conceptual' and 'metaphysical' should not be thought of as marking a distinction in kinds of necessity and possibility, relates to what it was that convinced us (most of us) that 'Water = H_2O' is necessarily true, albeit a posteriori.

What convinced us were the arguments of Kripke and Putnam about how to *describe* certain possibilities, rather than arguments about what is possible *per se*. They convinced us that a world where XYZ is the watery stuff of our acquaintance did not warrant the description 'world where water is XYZ', and the stuff correctly described as water in a counterfactual world is the stuff—H_2O—which is the watery stuff of our acquaintance in the actual world be it watery or not in the counterfactual world.[33]

The key point is that the right way to describe a counterfactual world sometimes depends in part on how the actual world is, and

---

[33] Or, if we are considering the 'same world' version of the Twin Earth parable, they convinced us that a remote location where XYZ is the watery stuff did not warrant the description 'location where water is XYZ'. It is, though, the 'other world' version of Twin Earth that matters for the debate over the necessary a posteriori. It was, of course, Putnam who put the point in terms of Twin Earth as such.

not solely on how the counterfactual world is in itself. The point is not one about the space of possible worlds in some newly recognized sense of 'possible', but instead one about the role of the actual world in determining the correct way to describe certain counterfactual possible worlds.

Scientific Thought Experiments

I have just said that the famous Twin Earth parable tells us something about how to describe certain possibilities. Many insist that this is quite the wrong way, and indeed far too deflationary a way, to read the parable. They insist that it should be regarded instead as a scientific thought experiment of a kind with those made famous (and respectable) by, among others, Galileo, Newton, and Einstein.

This is hard to believe. The famous thought experiments in science seek to establish certain rather general results about the nature of the world around us. Newton sought to prove the existence of absolute space; Einstein sought to show that there is no privileged inertial frame; and Galileo exposed a tension between common sense and two laws of Aristotelian physics.

Take, for example, a simple version of Galileo's famous, lovely thought experiment. According to Aristotelian physics, the greater the mass, the faster a body falls, so a mass of thirty grams will fall more quickly than a mass of twenty grams, which in turn will fall more quickly than a mass of ten grams. Also, according to Aristotelian physics, naturally slow-moving things attached to naturally fast moving things will slow the faster moving things down. Thus a mass of twenty grams with a mass of ten grams attached to it will fall more slowly than a mass of twenty grams. But a mass of twenty grams with a mass of ten grams attached to it can be regarded as a mass of thirty grams, and so by the first principle should fall faster than either a mass of ten grams or a mass of twenty grams! Galileo showed by this line of reasoning that two laws of Aristotelian physics are in conflict with our common-sense conviction that a mass of ten grams attached to a mass of twenty grams can be regarded as a mass of thirty grams when predicting physical behaviour. We thereby learnt something about what our world is like. We should not be too surprised at thought experiments revealing facts about the empirical world. Detective stories make us familiar with the idea that reconstructing 'in our minds' what would have been involved in the butler doing it may reveal that he could not have done it. This is surely very different from what we learn from the Twin Earth thought experiments. They do not lead us to revise our views about what Earth is like, or indeed what Twin Earth is fundamentally like.

I know from experience that many find this too deflationary a response to the Twin Earth parable. The issue, runs a common protest, is one about essential properties and not one about word usage. My best guess about the source of this protest is a conflation of the question of the essential properties of water with the question of what is essential for being water. It is easy to be seduced by the following argument:

Pr. 1   Water is H_2O. (Agreed fact which is also agreed to be a posteriori)

Pr. 2 H_2O is essentially H_2O. (Agreed fact about essential properties)

Conc.   It is necessary a posteriori that water is H_2O

into thinking that the necessary a posteriori nature of 'Water is H_2O' has nothing to do with the right occasions for using the term 'water'. For neither premiss in the above argument makes any reference to word usage. But consider the following argument:

Pr. 1   Our main example is H_2O. (Agreed fact which is also agreed to be a posteriori)

Pr. 2 H_2O is essentially H_2O. (Agreed fact about essential properties)

Conc.   It is necessary a posteriori that our main example is H_2O.

The conclusion of this argument is false. We might have chosen as our main example heat/molecular kinetic energy instead of water/H_2O. The moral is that it is crucial to the necessary status of 'Water is H_2O' that the word 'water' is, unlike 'our main example', a rigid designator. And what reveals that 'water' is a rigid designator are our intuitions about how to *describe* Twin Earth.

Reply to a Methodological Objection

I have argued against the two senses view, the view that we need to distinguish conceptual from metaphysical possibilities, by arguing that we can explain the phenomena thought to require the distinction in terms of a single space of possibilities of the weakest or most inclusive kind, whatever exactly that may be. The methodological objection is that possibility and necessity are, at bottom, properties of *sentences*, and when we look at sentences the plain fact is that there is an important difference between the sentences 'If H_2O covers most of the Earth, water covers most of the Earth' and 'If H_2O covers most of the Earth, H_2O covers most of the Earth'.

I think we should reject the view that necessity and possibility are at bottom properties of sentences. Sentences *qua* sentences are physical structures that serve to represent how things are. In this regard they are not different in kind from drawings, flags at half mast, certain gestures, and so on. They get to be objects of interest when we discuss possibility and necessity only in as much as they have interpretations—that is, can be viewed as standing for ways things might be or possibilities. Thus, it seems to me, we should regard as fundamental the question of how many kinds of possibility we need to distinguish, not how many kinds of sentence; therefore, if we can handle the manifest difference between 'If H_2O covers most of the Earth, then water covers most of the Earth' and 'If H_2O covers most of the Earth, then H_2O covers most of the Earth' in terms of a single class of possibilities, this shows we should be 'one-sensers' about conceptual versus metaphysical possibility and necessity.

It is, of course, a fair challenge to this position to point out that sentences are more ontologically respectable than possibilities. But, as we noted in Chapter 1, first, there are a number of extant accounts of possibilities to choose from, and secondly, we need an account of possibilities in any case—as economists, phase state physicists, theorists of information and representation, and even the folk planning their holidays, well know.

The Question of A Priori Deducibility

My reply to the objection from the distinction between conceptual and metaphysical possibility is now before you. It is that the distinction does not show that we need to acknowledge two senses of possibility and necessity, and so does not show that we should do all our discussions of global supervenience theses twice over: once with the theses quantifying over conceptual possibilities, and once with them quantifying over metaphysical possibilities. But the *question* we mentioned at the beginning remains. Once we acknowledge that there are necessary a posteriori sentences, we can and should ask whether the physicalists' commitment to entailments from sentences about the physical way things are, to the psychological way they are, leads to a commitment to conceptual entailments from the physical to the psychological, to a priori conditionals linking the physical way things are to the psychological way things are.

If the explanation drawing on two-dimensional modal logic we gave above of the necessary a posteriori is correct, the answer to our question is that physicalists' are committed to the existence of conceptual entailments from the physical to the psychological.[34] The point can be most easily made with an example.

Consider the relation between the H_2O way the world is and the water way it is. The former entails the latter, and you might naturally think that no entailment from the H_2O way things are to the water way they are could possibly be a conceptual entailment. For instance,

(2) H_2O covers most of the Earth;

(3) Therefore, water covers most of the Earth

is valid in the sense that every world where the premiss is true is a world where the conclusion is true,[35] but, of course, the

---

[34] Hence, on one understanding of what it is to be a *reductive* physicalist, physicalists should be reductive physicalists. But remember our earlier example of sentences about average house sizes. We might, reasonably enough, say that facts about average house sizes are *reducible* to facts about individual house sizes on the ground that the truth about average house sizes is a priori deducible from enough information about individual house sizes. But we might, not perhaps as reasonably but nevertheless with some justification, deny reducibility on the ground that we cannot even in principle write down the necessary and sufficient conditions for sentences about average house sizes in terms of ones about individual houses.

[35] Assuming we are quantifying over counterfactual worlds. In other words, every world where the C-proposition associated with (2)—the proposition expressed by (2)—is true is a world where the C-proposition associated with (3)—the proposition expressed by (3)—is true.

conditional with the premiss as antecedent and the conclusion as consequent is necessary a posteriori, not a priori. However, if the two-dimensional account of the necessary a posteriori is correct, the explanation for the a posteriori nature of the conditional is that understanding alone does not give the proposition expressed by the conditional sentence, that is, does not give the C-proposition associated with the conditional sentence. What understanding alone does give, though, is the way the proposition expressed depends on context, on the relevant facts outside the head, on the relevant facts about how things actually are. Thus, if the two-dimensional explanation of the necessary a posteriori is correct, the appropriate supplementation of the premisses by contextual information will give a set of premisses that do lead a priori to the conclusion. We will be able to move a priori from, for example, sentences about the distribution of H_2O *combined* with the right context-giving statements, to the distribution of water. And exactly this is true for the inference just given, for consider:

(2) H_2O covers most of the Earth;

(2a) H_2O is the watery stuff of our acquaintance;

(3)   Therefore, water covers most of the Earth.

Although the passage from (2) to (3) is a posteriori, the passage from (2) together with (2a) to (3) is a priori in view of the a priori status of 'Water is the watery stuff of our acquaintance'. Although our understanding of the sentence 'Water covers most of the Earth' does not in itself give the proposition it expresses, it does give the proposition it expresses when we know the context and (2a) gives the context, for it gives the relevant fact about us and our world.[36] Indeed, (2a) records the a posteriori, contingent fact we needed to discover to know that (2) entailed (3): we did not know that (2) entailed (3) until we learnt (2a). But as soon as we learnt (2a), we had the wherewithal to move a priori from (2) *together* with (2a), to (3).

---

[36] I assume the particular reference-fixing story told earlier for 'water', about, that is, the *A*-intension of 'water'. Other views about how the reference-fixing story should go would require appropriately different versions of (2a). Although any view about how 'water' gets to pick out what it does will be controversial, it is incredible that there is *no* story to tell—it is not magic that 'water' picks out what it does pick out—so we can be confident that there is a reference-fixing story to tell.

The crucial point here is the way that the contextual information, the relevant information about how things actually are, by virtue of telling us in principle the propositions expressed by the various sentences (or, equivalently, the C-propositions associated with them) enables us to move a priori from the H_2O way things are to the water way they are. But if physicalism is true, all the information needed to yield the propositions being expressed about what the actual world is like in various physical sentences can be given in physical terms, for the actual context is givable in physical terms according to physicalism. Therefore, physicalism is committed to the in principle a priori deducibility of the psychological from the physical.

A Simple Argument to Finish With

The argument just given rests on a view about the necessary a posteriori that, because of its very subject-matter, is inevitably controversial. So let me conclude this chapter by pointing out that there is a much shorter way of making plausible the view that physicalism is committed to the a priori deducibility of psychological nature from physical nature.

It is implausible that there are facts about very simple organisms that cannot be deduced a priori from enough information about their physical nature and how they interact with their environments, physically described. The physical story about amoebae and their interactions with their environments is the whole story about amoebae. Of course, if there is a necessary a posteriori truth, *Tr,* that cannot be known a priori from the full physical story about the world, *pace* what I have just said physicalists are committed to, we can 'grue' up a property 'of' amoebae that cannot be a priori deduced, namely, that of being a *Tr*-amoeba, where x is a *Tr*-amoeba if and only if x is an amoeba and *Tr*. But this will not be in any interesting sense a property *of* amoebae. Now, according to physicalism, we differ from amoebae essentially only in complexity of ingredients and their arrangement. It is hard to see how that kind of difference could generate important facts about us that in principle defy our powers of deduction. Think of the charts in biology classrooms showing the evolutionary progression from single-celled organisms on the far left to the higher apes and humans on the far right: where in that progression can the physicalist plausibly claim that failure of a priori deducibility of important facts about these organisms and creatures emerges? Or, if it comes to that, where in the development of each and every one of us from a zygote could the physicalist plausibly locate the place where there emerge important facts about us that cannot in principle be deduced from the physical story about us? But facts about our psychology are important facts about us, so the physicalist, on pain of embracing what we might call emergentism with respect to the necessary a posteriori, is committed to the a priori deducibility of psychological nature from physical nature.

AFTERWORD ON METAPHYSICAL VERSUS CONCEPTUAL NECESSITY

'There is a clear distinction between "All water is water" and "All water is H_2O", often marked by saying that the first is conceptually necessary and the second is metaphysically necessary. You hold that there are not two sorts of necessity, and tell a complicated story about sentences, understanding, and *A*-versus *C*-intensions and propositions, but where, after all is said and done, do you stand on the clear distinction between "All water is water" and "All water is H_2O"?'

Fair question. Here is my reply.

It is crucial to be clear about whether the question is being asked about the sentences or about the propositions associated with the sentences. Sentences get to have semantic properties like being true or necessary in as much as they bear interpretations. The physical structure types and tokens *per se* do not have semantic properties. And in as much as they have interpretations, they have truth-conditions under those interpretations, or at least they do if they are to be candidates for necessary *truth*. (It may, *may*, be that conditionals and ethical sentences have interpretations that do not confer truth-conditions.) So let's consider the question first as asked of the sets of truth-conditions—that is, the propositions in the coarse-grained sense of 'proposition' we have been using—associated with the sentences in English.

I say—in good though controversial company (Tichy, Lewis, Stalnaker, Chalmers, among others)—that there are *two* propositions associated with 'All water is water', and with 'All water is H_2O': the A-proposition/intension and the C-proposition/intension, as I called them, of the sentences. Others have different names for essentially the same distinction. Now the C-intension of 'All water is water' is identical with the C-intension of 'All water is H_2O', so 'they' have the same modal and epistemic status: in particular, the C-intension in question is necessary, and, plausibly, a priori . It is the C-intension that people most often have in mind, naturally enough, when they talk of the proposition *expressed* by a sentence, and what I am saying in this terminology is that the proposition expressed by 'All water is water' and the proposition expressed by 'All water is H_2O' is one and the same, namely, the set of all worlds, so there cannot be any difference in modal or epistemic status.

On the other hand, the A-intension of 'All water is water' is distinct from the A-intension of 'All water is H_2O'. The first is the same set as the C-intension of 'All water is water'. However, the A-intension of 'All water is H_2O' is a proper subset of that set of all worlds, and is straightforwardly contingent and a posteriori.

Suppose now we ask our question of the sentences *qua* interpreted sentences of English. The answer will depend on whether we go by the status of the A- or C-intensions when we assign modal properties to the sentences. If, as is usual and natural, and as I did in this chapter, we go by the status of C-intensions, the status of the propositions expressed, both 'All water is water' and 'All water is H_2O' have the *same* modal status; if we go by the modal status of the A-intensions, the first is necessary and the second is contingent; and, finally, if we insist that it would be misleading not to tell the fuller story, we say that there is no single answer, rather, we must say that the sentences have the same C-intension, an intension that is necessary (and arguably a priori), but different A-intensions, one being necessary and the other contingent.

Finally, there is the question of how a *sentence* might count as necessary a posteriori. Because understanding delivers A-intensions, and whether A-intensions are distinct from C-intensions, but does not deliver C-intensions, if you assign modal status by the status of C-intensions, 'All water is H_2O' will be an example of a necessarily true sentence whose modal status is not revealed by understanding alone. This is the sense in which the sentence counts as necessary a posteriori. By way of contrast, as the A-intension of both 'All water is water' and 'All H_2O is H_2O' is the universal set and is the same as their C-intension, in their case understanding alone reveals their necessary modal status (and this remains true, of course, if you insist that to count as necessary a sentence must have a necessary A-intension in *addition* to a necessary C-intension). They, accordingly, do not count as necessary a posteriori.

We can do the same 'divide and elucidate' exercise on the claim that it is epistemically possible that some water is not H_2O. The C-proposition associated with 'Some water is not H_2O' is not epistemically possible, but the A-proposition is—being in fact contingent and a posteriori. The *sentence* 'Some water is not H_2O' is epistemically possible in the following sense: consistent with what is required to understand it, the sentence might have expressed something both false and discoverable to be false: that is to say, its A-proposition is consistent with the context determining a false and knowably false C-proposition, though the C-proposition it in fact expresses is necessarily false.

In the next chapter, we 'dirty our hands'. I offer an account of how to place colour in the physical picture of what our world is like that draws on the methodology defended and explained in the first three chapters.

CHAPTER 4

The Primary Quality View of Colour

The Location Problem for Colour

THERE is an important sense in which we know the live possibilities as far as colour is concerned. We know that objects have dispositions to look one or another colour, that they have dispositions to modify incident and transmitted light in ways that underlie their dispositions to look one or another colour, that they have physical properties that are responsible for both these dispositions, and that subjects have experiences as of things looking one or another colour. We also know that this list includes all the possibly relevant properties. Some say that the completeness of this list is an empirical discovery of science; others that the view that it might have turned out that redness, say, is a feature of reality additional to, and different in kind from, those listed—a non-dispositional, intrinsic feature of surfaces quite distinct from their physical properties—is some kind of conceptual confusion. Either way, the list is complete. Also, we have words for the listed properties—I used them in giving the list. But these words are not colour names as such; they are rather terms for dispositions to look coloured and affect light, for the physical property bases of these dispositions, and for certain perceptual experiences. Colour thus presents a classic example of the location problem. The colours must, if they are instantiated anywhere, be findable somehow, somewhere in accounts that mention dispositions to look coloured and affect light, the physical bases of these dispositions, and colour experiences; it must be the case that some of these properties have colour names as well as names from our list. Our question is, which ones?

My answer is the 'Australian' view that colours are physical properties of objects: certain physical properties of objects have colour names as well as their physical property names. This view is sometimes known as the primary quality view of colour, although the idea is not that colours are identical with complexes of primary qualities in a sense tied to Locke's famous list, but rather that they are identical with complexes of certain of the properties the physical sciences appeal to, or will appeal to, in their causal explanations of things' looking coloured.

How might you argue for this view, or indeed for any view about which properties are named by the colour terms? You might, of course, stipulate that in your mouth the word 'red', say, names the disposition to look red, or perhaps that it names the relevant feature of the experience that we call something's looking red to one, but that would hardly address the question of which property the word 'red' names in the mouths of others, and, more generally, in the mouths of the folk. In order to address that question, we need to start with what we find most obvious about colour. Accordingly, I start by emphasizing what seems most obvious about colour, the fact that is sufficiently central to count as defining our subject. We will see how this fact, when combined with what science tells us, forces us to identify colours with certain physical properties. I then note some properties of the resulting account of colour, including how it accommodates what is right about the dispositional view of colour. The final part of the chapter is concerned with certain well-known objections to the primary quality view that arise, as is only proper given our starting-point, from folk views about colour that seem, when combined with certain empirical facts, to be inconsistent with identifying colours with physical properties.

THE PRIME INTUITION ABOUT COLOUR

The Visually Conspicuous Nature of the Colours

There is something peculiarly visually conspicuous about the colours. Redness is visually presented in a way that having inertial mass and being fragile, for instance, are not. When we teach the meanings of the colour words, we aim to get our hearers to grasp the fact that they are words for the properties putatively presented in visual experience when things look coloured. By contrast, the term 'square' picks out a property that is *only* visually conspicuous in objects that are coloured (in the wide sense in which anything not completely transparent is coloured).

However, although colours present themselves in visual experience in a peculiarly conspicuous way, we do not use 'red' as the name of the experience itself, but rather of the property of the object putatively experienced when it looks red. For we examine objects to determine their colour; we do not introspect. We look out, not in. Moreover, we hold objects up to the light and look carefully before ruling on their colour; and we regard the opinions of others, particularly others visually better placed than we are, as relevant to arriving at the right judgement concerning an object's colour. In sum, the ways we arrive at judgements about the colours of objects have the distinctive hallmarks of the ways we arrive at judgements about the nature of the objects we interact with. Our judgements of colour seek to conform themselves to the nature of these objects, despite the fact the colour an object seems to have has special authority in determining the colour it is.

We can sum this up by saying that some such clause as:

> 'red' denotes the property of an object putatively presented in visual experience when that object looks red

is a subject-determining platitude for red. Let's call this platitude, and the corresponding platitudes for yellow, green, and so on, the prime intuition about colour. The prime intuition is simply that red is the property objects look to have when they look red—and if this sounds like a triviality, as surely it does, that is all to the good. It is evidence that we have found a secure starting-place.

Causation and Presentation

Despite its trivial sound, our prime intuition tells us something important about the metaphysics of colour when we combine it with plausible views about what is required for an experience to be the presentation of a property.

The question: How must experience E be related to property P to count as the presentation of P, or, equivalently, to count as E representing in experience that something is P? is a notoriously difficult one. Nevertheless, part of the story is relatively uncontroversial. A necessary condition for E to be the presentation of P is that there be a causal connection in normal cases. Sensations of heat are the way heat, that is, molecular kinetic energy in the case of objects whose molecules move, typically presents itself to us; and essential to this is the fact that molecular kinetic energy typically causes sensations of heat in us.

What is controversial is what is sufficient for E to be the presentation of P. We know that mere causal connection is not enough: there are far too many normal causes of any given experience. However, for present purposes we can largely set to one side the hard question of what has to be added to causation to get presentation. We can work with the rough schema: redness is the property of objects which typically causes them to look red in the right way, where the phrase 'the right way' is simply code for whatever is needed to bring causation up to presentation, for whatever is needed to make the right selection from the very many normal causes of a thing's looking red. In particular, the rough schema gives us enough to show that the dispositional theory of colour is mistaken, or so I will now argue.

THE CASE AGAINST THE DISPOSITIONAL THEORY OF COLOUR

Background on Causation

Before I present the case against the dispositional theory of colour based on the prime intuition, we need to note that properties can be causes.

How things are at one time causally affects how things are at future times. How much coffee I drink at dinner affects how much sleep I get that night; the film *The Way We Were* is about how the way its protagonists were in their youth led to how they became in middle age; how steep an incline is, is responsible for how short of breath a climber is; and so on and so forth. But talk of how things are is talk of properties; thus, to the (considerable) extent that these examples strike us as commonplaces, it is a commonplace that causation relates properties.

A good question is how to integrate this commonplace into the familiar events framework for thinking about causation. We might construe events (in the sense relevant to causation) as property-like entities. Or we might distinguish two kinds of things that can stand in causal relations: events considered as concrete entities to be placed in the category of particulars, and, secondly, certain properties of these events. There would then be two subjects for discussion: which events cause which events, and which properties of these events are responsible for their standing in these causal relations. For it is because of the properties the events have that they stand in the causal relations that they do stand in, and, moreover, we can distinguish which properties of some cause-event matter for which properties of some effect-event—the steepness of the incline matters for how short of breath the climber is, but the colour of my sweater is neither here nor there.

It does not matter for our purposes which strategy is the right one. What matters is that properties are causes, however this fact should be integrated into our talk of events causing events.[1] With this background we can now present the case against the dispositional theory of colour.

Dispositions are not Causes

The dispositional theory of colour is mistaken because dispositions are not causes, and, in particular, are not causes of their manifestations. Their categorical bases do all the causing, where by the categorical basis of a disposition in some object, I mean the property of the object responsible for its having the disposition; that is, the property that is responsible for the object's being disposed to behave in the way definitive of the disposition in question. Consider, to illustrate the point, a fragile glass that shatters on being dropped because it is fragile, and not (say) because of some peculiarity in the way it is dropped. Suppose that it is a certain kind of bonding B between the glass molecules which is responsible for the glass being such that if dropped, it breaks. Then the dispositional

---

[1] I here skate over a large debate. For further references and more argument for the view I favour, see Frank Jackson, 'Essentialism, Mental Properties and Causation', *Proceedings of the Aristotelian Society*, 95 (1995): 253–68. For a recent statement of the other side, see Donald Davidson, 'Thinking Causes', in John Heil and Al Mele, eds., *Mental Causation* (Oxford: Clarendon Press, 1993), 3–17. Of course, when I say that properties are causes I do not mean that property *universals* are causes. When the squareness of a child's building block causes it to bump when rolled, the squareness of *my table* has nothing to do with it. I mean that how things are at certain times and places are causes.

property of being fragile is the second-order property of having some first-order property or other, bonding *B* as we are supposing, that is responsible for the glass being such as to break when dropped. And the first-order property, bonding *B*, is the categorical basis of the fragility. But then it is bonding *B*, together with the dropping, that causes the breaking; there is nothing left for the second-order property (second-order in the sense of being the property of having a property), the disposition itself, to do. All the causal work is done by bonding *B* in concert with the dropping. To admit the fragility also as a cause of the breaking would be to admit a curious, ontologically extravagant kind of overdetermination.[2] Or consider what happens when a signal is amplified by an amplifier. Surely what causes the signal to increase is not the amplifier's being an amplifier, but rather whatever features the amplifier's designers put into it that make it an amplifier.

Peter Menzies has pointed out that cases where different dispositions have the same basis raise a problem here.[3] A well-known example is the opacity and electrical conductivity of many metals. The basis for the different dispositional properties of opacity and conductivity is, roughly, the way free electrons permeate the metal; nevertheless, an explanation in terms of a metal's opacity is clearly not the same as one in terms of its conductivity. For instance, the behaviour of a galvanometer would not normally be explained by the opacity of a metal rod, but might well be explained by its conductivity. But I have to say that the cause is the same in both cases, so how can I account for the difference in explanation? I have to

---

[2] The thesis that dispositional properties, and functional properties in general, are not causes has been much discussed recently in connection with the question of the causal efficacy of content, see e.g. Ned Block, 'Can the Mind Change the World', in G. Boolos, ed., *Meaning and Method: Essays in Honor of Hilary Putnam* (Cambridge: Cambridge University Press, 1990), and Frank Jackson and Philip Pettit, 'Functionalism and Broad Content', *Mind*, 97 (1988): 381–400. I set aside what to say about the causal role of 'bare' dispositions, if such are possible. All the dispositions we are concerned with here are not bare; they all have bases to cause their manifestations.

[3] In discussion; the example is David Lewis's in another context. Ned Block has objected (in correspondence) that cases where different dispositions appear to have the same basis, and, more generally, cases where different functional roles appear to be occupied by the same state, turn out, on examination, to involve subtly different bases and states. But it would be strange if having learnt the lesson of multiple realizability that the same role may be filled by different states, we turned around and insisted that the converse—different roles filled by the same state—is impossible.

say that when we explain by citing a disposition, we are doing two things together: we are saying that the basis of the disposition, be it known or not, did the causing, and that what got caused has a special connection with the manifestation of the disposition. When conductivity explains the behaviour of the galvanometer, the behaviour of the galvanometer will have a special connection to a manifestation of conductivity that it lacks to any manifestation of opacity; this is why it is right to cite conductivity, and wrong to cite opacity, as the explanation of the galvanometer's behaviour. Thus, we cite electrical conductivity as the explanation when a current flow plays a special role in the path to what happens, and cite opacity when a failure of light to pass through something plays a special role in the causal path to what happens.

It follows, therefore, from the prime intuition that the colours are presented in colour experience, and so are causes or potential causes of things' looking one or another colour, that the colours are not dispositions to look coloured. They are instead the categorical bases of dispositions to look coloured. Moreover, the categorical bases of the dispositions are, we know, one or another complex of physical properties of the objects, perhaps in conjunction with their surroundings.

We can spell the argument out thus:

Pr. 1   Yellowness is the property of objects putatively presented to subjects when those objects look yellow. (Prime intuition)

Pr. 2   The property of objects putatively presented to subjects when the objects look yellow is at least a normal cause of their looking yellow. (Conceptual truth about presentation)

Pr. 3   The only causes (normal or otherwise) of objects' looking yellow are complexes of physical qualities. (Empirical truth)

Conc.   Yellowness is a complex of the physical qualities of objects.

And likewise for all the colours.

The obvious analogy is with heat. Feelings of heat are the putative presentations in perceptual experience of heat. Thus, heat is not the disposition to cause *inter alia* sensations of heat, but rather what causes the sensations of heat and the various phenomena associated with heat. But what does the causing in the right way is molecular kinetic energy. Thus, heat is molecular kinetic energy.[4]

Are the Bases Themselves Dispositions?

Bill Lycan (among many) has objected that there is no interesting distinction in kind between 'categorical' basis and disposition, and, more generally, between what occupies a functional role and the functional role occupied.[5] When we specify what fills a functional role, we simply specify some further functional property. Suppose, for example, we find that the causal basis for the disposition to look yellow in some object is a certain surface molecular configuration. Aren't molecules, Lycan would ask, in part defined in terms of the *role* they play in physical theory? Moreover, a molecular configuration can be multiply realized. Many different arrangements of molecules and their sub-molecular constituents will make up the same configuration. But, first, the question of the nature of some property is distinct from the question of the nature of the language we may use to pick it out. Non-functional and non-dispositional properties can be, and very often are, picked out via what they do—for example, in the words 'the body shape that disposes to heart attacks'. Any specification of the causal basis of the disposition to look yellow that colour science comes up with will most likely contain dispositional and functional terms—they are endemic—but it does not follow that the basis is itself a disposition. Secondly, there are two distinct senses in which a state or property may be multiply realized. The multiple realisability distinctive of dispositional and functional properties is a matter of the possibility of a number of different states doing the very same causal job. This is quite different from the fact that nearly all states are multiply realizable in the sense that they can be regarded as being, to some degree or other, disjunctive, and, accordingly, as realizable by virtue of one or another disjunct obtaining. The body

---

[4] I follow the usual 'convention' of ignoring molecular potential energy, and generally of grossly simplifying the science.

[5] William G. Lycan, *Consciousness* (Cambridge, Mass.: MIT Press, 1987), see ch. 4.

shape that disposes to heart attacks can be realized in many ways, but this does not mean that shape is a dispositional or functional property.

SOME FEATURES OF THE PRIMARY QUALITY VIEW OF COLOUR

I now note some properties of the primary quality account, and most especially how it accommodates the data that so famously point towards the dispositional theory, before we turn to a consideration of three objections to it.

First, the primary quality account should regard attributions of colour as *relativized to a kind of creature and a circumstance of viewing*. The primary quality account is the result of combining a causal theory of colour—the view that the colours are the properties that stand in the right causal connections to our colour experiences—with empirical information about what causes colour experiences. And a causal theory of colour takes as fundamental: colour for a kind of creature in a circumstance.

The relativity to kinds of creatures arises from the fact that which properties of the world around us stand in the right relations to certain experiences for those experiences to count as presentations of the properties is, in part, a matter of how the creatures having the experiences are, just as which kinds of intruders a burglar alarm latches onto is in part a matter of how the alarm is made, and which weather conditions a barometer records is in part a matter of how the barometer is calibrated.

The relativity to circumstances of viewing arises from the fact that the very same thing may look different colours in different circumstances, and yet there may be no substantial reason to favour one appearance over the other. For example, the coloured patches in many magazines look red from normal viewing distances but are revealed as made up of small magenta and yellow dots on closer inspection.[6] Some insist that the red appearance is an illusion. The patches are really magenta and yellow. This response faces two problems. First, it means that we are under illusion much

---

[6] I take the example from Mark Johnston, 'How to Speak of the Colors', *Philosophical Studies*, 68 (1992): 221–63.

more often than we naturally suppose. A lot of things look very different colours when viewed close up. Secondly, it is hard to say in any non-arbitrary way what the right viewing circumstances for the 'real' colour of an object are, and yet we know that just about any object will look different colours depending on how closely it is viewed. Famously, blood does not look red under a microscope, and nothing looks any colour under an electron microscope. Moreover, the situation is quite different from one in which a change of circumstance actually affects the object seen in some significant way. Then the right thing to say is that the object changes colour as we go from one circumstance to the other—the situation is, in principle, no different from what happens when we paint a white object red, except that the viewing circumstance 'does' the painting. But the coloured patches in the magazines do not alter as we viewers peer more closely at them. Nor does blood change when viewed through a microscope. What we need to say, accordingly, is that the colour something has in—in the sense of relative to—one circumstance may differ from the colour it has in another, where viewing distance is part of the circumstance, and that each colour is equally 'real'.

In any case this is what the causal theory must do. For it is plausible that both the looking red from a normal viewing distance and the looking made-up-of-yellow-and-magenta-dots from close up are colour experiences that count as presentations of features of what is seen. Although what must be added to causation in order to get presentation is controversial, there is a fair degree of agreement about the general shape of what is needed. We need clauses requiring that there be a systematic dependence between the nature of the experience and the nature of what is experienced, a dependence that allows us to think of the experience as tracking the nature of what is experienced, and it is plausible that there will be such dependencies both between the red-look at a reasonable distance and a patch's surface, and between the assemblies-of-yellow-and-magenta-dots look from close up and (some different feature of) the patch's surface.[7]

In sum, the causal theory should take as basic: colour for S in circumstance C, as is made explicit in the following schema:

---

[7] And, for those who like teleological theories of content, we could add the relevant observations about selectional history.

> O is red at *t* for *S* in *C* iff there is a property *P* of *O* at *t* that typically interacts with *S* in circumstances *C* to cause *O* to look red in the right way for that experience to count as the presentation of *P* to *S*.

As we are humans, we are naturally interested in redness for humans, and for humans whose perceptual faculties are working normally or properly—just as we are more interested in poisons for humans (what is poisonous for us) than in poisons for Martians (what is poisonous for them). Thus, we typically count things as red just if they have a property that interacts with normal humans to make the objects look red in such a way that their so looking counts as the presentation of the property to normal humans. Also, there is a wide range of circumstances we count as normal for viewing the world, in the sense of being circumstances that reveal the nature of it to us. For instance, seeing something from somewhere between a third of a metre and ten metres, in daylight during most parts of the day, or in typical indoor lighting, are all good for detecting the shape, distance away, size and relative position of the objects around us, and it is the colour of objects in such normal circumstances that especially interests us. We know that visual perception in these circumstances tells us more about the nature of the objects around us than what happens when we look at them at dusk, or from a kilometre away, say. Moreover, mostly objects look much the same colour in all the circumstances we count as normal. The aforementioned coloured patches are something of an exception. Accordingly, from now on I will be concerned principally with colour in a thoroughly anthropocentric sense tied to normal humans in normal circumstances. Thus, we can mostly work in terms of the following clause:

> O is red at *t* iff there is a property *P* of *O* at *t* that typically interacts with normal human perceivers in normal circumstances to make something that has it look red in the right way for that experience to count as the presentation of *P* in that object,

and its partners for the other colours. But the fact remains that the fundamental notion is that of the colour of O at T for S in C.[8]

---

[8] As far as I know, there are not equally good candidates for being normal human percipients whose colour perceptions deliver sharply different answers as to

Secondly, the clause specifying when something is red can be thought of as a piece of *reference-fixing* or as piece of *meaning-giving*.[9] If it is a piece of reference-fixing, the question of whether an object is red in some counterfactual world will turn on whether it has redness the way things actually are—that is, has a property which makes things look red in the right way in the actual world. If the clause is a piece of meaning-giving, what matters is what the property does in the counterfactual world—to be red in a world is to have a property that makes things look red in the right way in that world. I suspect that speakers of natural language vacillate between these two readings, depending in part on the persuasive powers of the philosophy tutor they are discussing the issue with. In either case, we can think of our clause as a priori, and its a priori nature constitutes our honouring of the commitment to the relativity of colour to viewers and circumstances.

Thirdly, the primary quality theory has an advantage over the dispositional theory of colour distinct from the causal advantage pressed earlier. For the primary quality theory can handle in a straightforward way a well-known problem for the dispositional theory.

The problem arises from cases where, by virtue of an object's relatively intrinsic nature, it would look a certain colour to persons with normal colour vision in normal circumstances, and yet it does not count as being that colour. There are many fanciful examples in the literature but here is one I owe to David Lewis; it is, by the standards that operate in philosophy, a real-life example. Suppose O has a surface property W that in itself would cause things to look white in the right way—perhaps the property is one that does the job in normal white paper. Suppose that O also has a

the colour of the objects around us. But if there are we would have to, on the appropriate occasions, relativize to one or another human percipient. If Jonathan Bennett, 'Substance, Reality, and Primary Qualities', repr. in C. B. Martin and D. M. Armstrong, eds., *Locke and Berkeley* (New York: Doubleday, 1968), pp. 86–124, is right about phenol-thio-urea, we do need to do this for taste. However, though phenol tastes bitter to about 75 per cent and is tasteless to about 25 per cent of otherwise comparable human tasters, the explanation may be (I understand) that what is being tasted is not phenol itself but a by-product produced only in certain mouths, in which case it is not true that one and the same substance has a dramatically different taste to equally normal tasters. Rather, one and the same substance causes different and different tasting substances in different mouths.

[9] Kripke, *Naming and Necessity*.

property that has no relevant effect on W except when O is in normal circumstances, but when it is, this 'stand-by' property S affects this property of O, perhaps by eliminating it or perhaps by modifying its normal action, in such a way that O looks black. In short, O is a piece of photo-sensitive paper—paper that is white in the dark but turns black on exposure to light.

What makes it true that the paper is white before exposure to light? Not the fact that it looks or would look white before exposure—before exposure it does not look any colour; and not the fact that it would look white were it seen in normal circumstances—as they involve exposure to light, it looks black in those circumstances. True, there is a short time lag before photo-sensitive paper turns black, but it is too short to see. (We may suppose—the example is only real-life by philosophical standards!) And yet clearly the paper is white before it is exposed to light. To say otherwise is to commit oneself implausibly to telling photographers who say that photo-sensitive paper *turns* black—and so was not black to start with—that they are wrong.

The primary quality theorist handles this example by drawing on the fact that there are two properties in play: property W of the paper's surface, and the stand-by property which operates very quickly, when normal viewing circumstances arrive. (If S *immediately* eliminates or modifies W—*per impossible*, as causation takes time in the real world—it is no longer intuitive that the paper is white until the normal circumstances arrive; we simply have a case where, though W by itself makes something white, the conjunction of W and S makes something black.) As long as the paper has an unmodified instance of W, the primary quality theorist can count it as white, because it has a property that normally disposes things to look white in normal circumstances. Thus, until the 'interfering' takes place, the paper counts as white. You might reasonably urge that this means that until W is eliminated or modified, the paper itself can be said to be disposed to look white in normal circumstances.[10] But the key point for us is that the story about why the

---

[10] Exactly what to say turns on how to handle 'finkish' dispositions—dispositions that tend to go away when the occasion for their manifestation arrives. These cases were raised many years ago by C. B. Martin, though, to my knowledge, he did not publish on the subject until his 'Dispositions and Conditionals', *Philosophical Quarterly*, 44 (1994): 1–8. For a response to the problem of finkish dispositions that would count the paper itself as disposed to look white until W is

paper counts as white until normal viewing circumstances arrive, turns on the role of the causal basis of the disposition, not on the question of whether the paper itself would look white in those normal viewing circumstances.

Fourthly, the primary quality theory can, as we said at the beginning, honour the dispositionalist's insight that there is something a priori, or somehow truistic, about the connection between being red and being appropriately disposed to look red.

Although the theory identifies colours with physical properties and so makes them objective and observer-independent, it is not an objective, observer-independent matter which physical properties (if any) are which colours. The basic idea can be illustrated with the example of the most dangerous chemical structure for humans. This structure is an objective, observer-independent property. For instance, on some ways of measuring toxicity it is, I understand, the structure of plutonium, and the structure of plutonium is an objective, observer-independent property. Nevertheless, what makes it true that plutonium is the most dangerous substance is of course a highly relative matter. It concerns the effect that plutonium has on humans, and that is in part a function of how humans are made. Likewise, on the causal theory of colour, which physical properties (if any) are which colours is an observer-dependent matter. It turns on whether the physical properties or property complexes in question have the right kinds of causal effects in the right kinds of ways on normal observers in normal circumstances to count as being presented in experience when things look one or another colour. David Hilbert has a good name for this kind of theory. He calls it *anthropocentric* realism.[11] The colours *per se* are observer-independent properties, but *which* observer-independent properties they are is not observer-independent.

What has masked the possibility of this kind of theory is the tendency to define the notion of a dispositional property in terms of the a priori nature of the relevant biconditional; to say, roughly, that Φ is a dispositional property iff some such biconditional as 'x is Φ iff x is of a nature such that x does such-and-such in so-and-so

eliminated or modified, see David Lewis, 'Finkish Dispositions', *Philosophical Quarterly*, 47 (1997), 143–58.

[11] David R. Hilbert, *Color and Color Perception: A Study in Anthropocentric Realism* (Stanford, Calif.: CSLI, 1987).

circumstances' is a priori.[12] But it is a priori that x has the most poisonous structure if and only if (roughly) x has a nature such that ingesting x has certain effects. Nevertheless, the most poisonous structure is not a disposition. It is the structure of plutonium.

What makes a property a disposition is that it itself is *essentially* linked to the production of certain results in certain circumstances, not whether some open sentence concerning it is a priori. And it is indeed a consequence of the causal theory that redness, for instance, is not essentially linked to looking red. Not just because of the possibility of 'defeaters', but because the, or any, property that typically makes things look red might fail to do so in some other world, just as the structure of plutonium might have been harmless to humans. In my role as a fence-sitter on whether the relevant causal roles (in part) fix the reference or give the meaning of the colour terms, I say nothing about whether things with these properties count as red in these worlds; what is clear and what matters for us is that the very properties that make things look red might not have.

Finally, I should note that the primary quality cum causal theory as presented here ducks an important issue. It refers to colour experiences under their colour-experience names, it says nothing illuminating about how to understand colour experience. Once upon a time I was convinced that any adequate account of colour experiences required reference to *qualia* understood as properties over and above those that appear in the physicalists' story about our world. Nowadays I am much more sympathetic to physicalism.

OBJECTIONS TO THE PRIMARY QUALITY THEORY

The primary quality theory of colour is built on the folk axiom that colours are the properties putatively presented in the experience of things looking coloured. The obvious question to ask then is whether there are other claims that are equally part of the folk theory of colour, and which, in one way or another, undermine the view that colours are physical properties. As I said at the beginning of this chapter, there is an important sense in which we know

---

12 Roughly—in view of the Martin point referred to in n. 10.

all the possibilities as far as colour is concerned—we know what the possibly relevant properties are, and we know how to name them—and the issue that remains is—to say it in Lewis-speak—which of the possibly relevant properties deserve the names of the colours in addition to the names they already have. And this is a question that can only be settled by consulting the folk theory of colour.

It has variously been suggested that the primary quality theory conflicts with (at least) three central tenets of the folk theory: the first is variously known as transparency or revelation, the idea that our experience of colour reveals its essential nature; the second is, in Keith Campbell's words, the axioms of unity;[13] and the third is the doctrine that different colours are strongly incompatible. The rest of this chapter will be mainly concerned with the first two suggested folk constraints on colour, and especially with whether they constitute objections to identifying the colours with physical properties. I will though say a little about strong incompatibility.

The Objection from Revelation

If colours are physical properties, it must be conceded that the way they look does not reveal their essential nature. When something looks red, it does not look one or another physical quality (or complex of physical qualities). You cannot see 'through' the experience to the nature of what is being experienced. Thus, if it is part of folk theory that the experience of colour reveals in itself the nature of colour, that colour is transparent in this sense, the primary property view must be false. And a number of philosophers have indeed suggested that it is part of the folk theory of colour that colour experience is transparent in the sense of revealing the essential nature of colour. For instance, Galen Strawson says that 'color words are *words for properties which are of such a kind that their whole and essential nature as properties can be and is fully revealed in sensory, phenomenal-quality experience, given only the qualitative character that that sensory experience has*'.[14] If

[13] Keith Campbell, 'Colours', in Robert Brown and C. D. Rollins, eds., *Contemporary Philosophy in Australia* (London: Allen & Unwin, 1969), 132–57.
[14] Galen Strawson, '"Red" and Red', *Synthese*, 78 (1989): 193–232, at 224, author's italics. Revelation is defended under the name of transparency by John

Strawson is right, colours, or at least colours as the folk conceive them, are not physical properties.

But is revelation really part of the folk theory of colour? There seem to me three reasons for denying that it is. First, it is hard to believe that our experience of colour is that different from our experience of heat. Perhaps before we had any idea of what heat was, some were tempted to say that sensations of heat revealed the full nature of heat, that heat is precisely that which is fully transparent to us when something feels hot. After all, that it feels hot was the main thing most people knew about heat, just as the main thing that is currently common knowledge about redness is that it makes things look red. However, our very preparedness to identify heat with molecular kinetic energy when the empirical evidence came in shows that this opinion was merely opinion. We did not hesitate to identify heat with something whose full nature is manifestly not given to us in the experience of heat.

Secondly, the folk allow that we can misperceive colour, that colour illusion is possible. But that is to draw a distinction between colours as they really are and colours as they appear to be, and that is to concede that the colours have a nature that outruns our experience of them.[15]

Finally, the prime intuition requires treating our experience of colour as typically caused by colour, and it is part of the folk notion of causation that causes and effects are distinct. But if our experience of colour is distinct from what it is an experience of, how could it transparently reveal the nature of colour? The folk thus know something about colour that tells them that revelation could not possibly be true. Of course, this last argument has force only if—unlike Mackie—we work on the general presumption that the folk are not badly confused.[16] If we incline to the view that the

Campbell, 'A Simple View of Colour', in John Haldane and Crispin Wright, eds., *Reality, Representation, and Projection* (New York: Oxford University Press, 1993), 257–68.

[15] A point made by Michael Smith, 'Colour, Transparency, Mind-Independence', in John Haldane and Crispin Wright, eds., *Reality, Representation, and Projection* (New York: Oxford University Press, 1993), 269–77.

[16] I have in mind Mackie's tendency to favour error theories that attribute to the folk seriously erroneous conceptions. See J. L. Mackie, *Ethics* (Harmondsworth: Penguin, 1977), for his error theory of (folk) value, and J. L. Mackie, *Problems from Locke* (Oxford: Clarendon Press, 1976), for his error theory of (folk) colour.

folk often are badly confused, a proponent of revelation can reply that here is an illustration of this very tendency to be confused. I think that the folk are smarter than that, but if you are of Mackie's mind, you can think of the last point as telling us how to restore consistency to the folk conception of colour: the way to do it is to drop revelation.

It might be suggested that although we should reject revelation, we should, nevertheless, try for a theory of colour that respects it as much as possible. Thus, Mark Johnston argues that the major advantage of a dispositional theory of colour over a primary quality theory—be it of our causalist variety or not—is that it gives enough to revelation to avoid sceptical worries that any primary quality theory necessarily engenders. He argues that the dispositional theory of colour secures an important cognitive value that the primary quality theory denies.

Vision can be a mode of revelation of the nature of visual response-dispositions. It cannot be a mode of revelation of the properties that the Primary Quality Theorist identifies with the colors. Since we are inevitably in the business of refiguring our inconsistent color concepts, we should make the revision which allows us to secure an important *cognitive value*—the value of acquaintance with those salient, striking and ubiquitous features that are the colors.

The point here is not simply that the Primary Quality Account does not satisfy even a qualified form of Revelation. What is more crucial is that as a result, the account does not provide for something we very much value: acquaintance with the colors. The ultimate defect of the Primary Quality View is therefore a *practical* one. From the point of view of what we might call the ethics of perception, the Secondary Quality Account is to be preferred. It provides for acquaintance with the colors.[17]

I think that this misunderstands the nature of the issue between primary quality cum causal theories and dispositional theories. There is, as we emphasized before, no deep metaphysical dispute between primary quality theorists and dispositionalists. The dispute is over whether the dispositions to look coloured or the physical quality bases of those dispositions should be tagged as the colours; the dispute is ultimately over the distribution of names among putative candidates. And how we answer this *labelling* question can have no cognitive, epistemic or practical significance.

---

[17] Johnston, 'How to Talk of the Colors', 258, my emphases.

If we reject revelation, we must reject the view that different colours are strongly incompatible in the sense of its being part of our very concept of different colours that they are *essentially* incompatible. *If* it is a priori that no object is red and green (all over, for a given S at a given time, and in a given circumstance), it will be because it is a priori that what is required by way of action (on S etc.) for an object to count as red all over (for S etc.) cannot co-exist with what is required by way of action (on S etc.) for an object to count as green all over (for S etc.). It will be like the impossibility of a substance being both poisonous and harmless to the very same population in the very same circumstances. But this is consistent with red and green themselves being compatible (though if they were ever together in an object, it would be wrong to call them 'red' and 'green'). What is ruled out by the denial of revelation is that it is a priori that the properties themselves are essentially incompatible, for that would require embracing some form of revelation into the essential nature of the colours. It may, of course, be a posteriori that red and green are essentially incompatible, but this is something primary quality theorists can happily accept. They can allow that it may turn out that the physical properties identical with red and green are mutually exclusive, as would be the case if one is having a 'grain' greater than x and the other is having a 'grain' less than x.

The Objection from the Axioms of Unity

The axioms of unity say that redness is the property common to all red things; that blueness is the property common to all blue things; and so on and so forth. If (a) the axioms of unity are a central part of the folk theory of colour, (b) a certain view about causation by disjunctive properties is correct, and (c) a certain empirical claim is correct, then the primary quality view is false.[18] Let me spell all this out.

Disjunctive properties can be causes. For instance, Tom's being taller than Dick may cause Tom to be chosen for the basketball team ahead of Dick. Equally, Tom's living next door to Dick may be the cause of Tom's knowing a lot about Dick. In both cases the cited cause can be thought of as disjunctive in the sense that it can

---

[18] I am indebted to Michael Watkins for pressing me on this point.

be realized in many different ways. Tom's being taller than Dick is a matter of Tom's being 200 cm and Dick's being 199 cm, or Tom's being 199 cm and Dick's being 198 cm, or . . .; and living next door can be thought of as a disjunction of the many significantly different ways of living next door. Indeed, it is arguable that most things we cite as causes are more or less disjunctive. When we cite the depth of the wound as responsible for the death of the victim, it is typically not the absolutely precise depth of the wound that matters but rather the fact that the wound's depth falls within a certain range of depths, any of which counts as deep. Nevertheless, excessively disjunctive properties cannot be causes. Indeed, we cannot even say that they are causes, properly speaking. Consider, for instance, the sentence 'Either arsenic administered by Harry or cyanide administered by Mary caused the death'. Surely we only make sense of this sentence by reading it as 'Either arsenic administered by Harry caused the death or cyanide administered by Mary caused the death'. When we are confronted with a claim that appears on the surface to cite an excessively disjunctive property as a cause, we make sense of it by reading the claim as one about one or another of the disparate disjuncts being the cause.

Now consider an example of Johnston's. Let us suppose that what makes a canary look yellow is a different property, P_1, from the property, P_2, that makes the relevant section of a colour photograph of the canary look yellow.[19] What should primary quality theorists identify as yellowness? The axioms of unity imply that they cannot say that P_1 is yellowness in the bird, whereas P_2 is yellowness in the area on the photograph. They must rather say that yellowness in both bird and photograph is the shared disjunction P_1 or P_2—or more generally that yellowness is the disjunction of all the physical property complexes that make things look yellow in the right way, but we will suppose that the disjunction of P_1 with P_2 covers all the cases.

Finally, suppose that P_1 and P_2 are very different, so different that the disjunction P_1 or P_2 counts as excessively disjunctive. Now the causal theory is in trouble. For it is built on the intuition that yellowness is what causes things to look yellow, and so cannot afford to identify yellowness with an excessively disjunctive property.

[19] Johnston, 'How to Speak of the Colors'.

How should we reply to the objection from the axioms of unity? We might follow Saul Kripke's lead and think of the colours as kinds. We might think of the word 'red' as denoting the kind K that a good number of exemplars of red things share and which causes them to look red (in the right way).[20] We then declare anything which is K, whether or not it looks red, to be red, and declare things which are not K but look red in normal circumstances to be 'fool's red'. Thus, if Johnston is right about the difference between what makes a canary look yellow and what makes the colour photograph of a canary look yellow, at least one of the canary and the photograph is fool's yellow. This approach might or might not be combined with the view that the colour terms are rigid designators. That is, we might understand

> 'red' denotes the (causally relevant) kind common to the red-looking exemplars of red things

as giving the meaning or as fixing the reference of 'red'. On the first understanding, the denotation specification applies world by world. The red things in a world w are the things that belong to the kind common to the red-looking exemplars of red things in w. But the red things in one world need not belong to the same kind as the red things in some other world. On the second understanding, 'red' is a rigid designator. The red things in a world w are the things that belong to the kind common to the red-looking exemplars of red things in the actual world, and so 'red' will denote the same kind in every world. (The latter is, I take it, what Kripke had in mind.)

I do not think that either version of the kind view is part of the folk theory of colour. Whether or not it turns out that there is some feature common to most things that look red, or most things that are, for whatever reason, counted as the exemplars of red things, a feature of sufficient note to count as marking out a kind which explains their looking red, I do not think our talk about red in any way presupposes that there is.

---

[20] See Kripke, *Naming and Necessity*, 128 n. 66 and 140 n. 71. Kripke's view is sometimes reported as that the colour terms mark out *natural* kinds. However, as Graham Oppy convinced me, it is not clear that he wants (or wanted at that time) to hold that all yellow things, say, have in common something significant enough to be regarded as collecting them into a natural kind.

In the case of terms like 'water' and 'gold' it is plausible that we take it for granted that there is something important that might be properly regarded as a kind, indeed a natural kind, distinctive of the exemplars of water and gold. As a result, the contention that it is part of their meaning that they denote kinds is plausible. But the diversity of kinds of things that look red—sunsets, ripe tomatoes, blood, feathers—along with the notorious variability of apparent colour, facts with which the folk have been long familiar, predispose the folk to expect that there may well not be any single kind distinctive of the things we use the word 'red' for. In short, the folk are too sensible to have presupposed something as risky as that there is a distinctive kind in common to things we call 'red'.

This is consistent with allowing that we might, after the event, give kind membership an important role in determining colour. Suppose it turns out that most of the things that look red to normal perceivers in normal circumstances do so because of some commonality that we may reasonably think of as marking out a kind. Then we might say that other things that look just as red to normal perceivers, in circumstances equally regardable as normal, but which are not of the kind in question, are fool's red.

The best reply to the objection from the axioms of unity is, I suggest, to urge that the disjunction is not excessively disjunctive. Even if most red things do not belong to a kind responsible for them normally looking red, there will turn out to be, all the same, sufficient similarity between what typically makes things look red to allow us to identify red with a disjunctive property that is sufficiently unified to count as a cause. For it is hard to believe that there is not enough rhyme or reason to things looking red given the evolutionary importance of colour vision, the role of colour difference in the detection of shape, the phenomenon of colour constancy (the fact that apparent colour is relatively invariant under changes in intensity of illumination), and the phenomenon of colour stability (the apparent colour of things in a given circumstance is fairly constant over time) to unify the disjunction. It makes good empirical sense that something physically interesting (which may well not have the status of marking out a kind except under extremely relaxed standards for kind-hood) unifies the various red-looking things over and above their being red-looking, and that colour vision is there in order to enable us to process this information, and that the same is true for the other colours.

It is sometimes thought an insuperable difficulty for this claim that we know that the physical nature of the light entering our eyes from objects that look the same colour varies greatly, and yet this physical nature is the relatively immediate cause of how the objects look. There is, it is said, no rhyme or reason to be found in the physical causes of one and the same colour judgement. For example, C. L. Hardin observes that 'apart from their radiative *result*, there is nothing that blue things have in common . . .'.[21] But consider an analogy pressed by Hilbert.[22] He points out that quite different factors are involved in our being able to see how far away things are. A major one is the information that comes from the fact that we have binocular vision, but you can still tell how far away things are with one eye closed or after losing the sight of one eye. This means that the very same judgement of visual depth may be driven by very different properties of the light that enters our eyes (and, if it comes to that, of the light that leaves the object). But it would be wrong to think that there is a disjunction problem here. The disparity in the nature of the light that enables us to make some given judgement of depth is irrelevant. What is relevant is the fact that there is a unifying distal property of the objects, namely, how far away they are, which our visual system disentangles from the otherwise disparate nature of the light it receives.

The issue then in the case of colour is whether there is a unifying distal property. Now there is some reason to hold that triples of integrated reflectances correlate closely with perceived colour. The fine detail is not important here, and, needless to say, it is controversial. But roughly a triple of integrated reflectances is the result of taking the reflectance—that is, certain proportions of reflected light to incident light—over three band-widths, scaling, and then summing. The result correlates closely with the apparent colour of reflecting surfaces.

What is more, these triples capture the similarity relations that are part of the folk theory of colour. The triple for orange, for instance, is closer to the triple for red than it is to the triple for blue. Hilbert infers that we should identify the colours with the relevant

[21] C. L. Hardin, 'Are "Scientific" Objects Coloured?', *Mind*, 93 (1984): 491–500, my emphasis.

[22] David R. Hilbert, 'What is Color Vision?', *Philosophical Studies*, 68 (1992): 351–70.

values of these triples, but here we have to be careful. Hilbert, as I understand him, thinks of the triples as themselves dispositional properties—as an object's disposition to reflect light displaying the relevant value of the triple. This is how he allows objects to have colours in the dark, and how he avoids having to say that light *creates* an object's colour rather than, as we folk want to say, *revealing* its colour. (There is no *actual* value of interest for the triple for an object in the dark.) But I cannot follow him in identifying the colours with these dispositions. I have to think of the value of the triple for a given colour, red, say, as what unifies the possibly highly disjunctive basis that is responsible for the disposition to look red in normal circumstances. It is what prevents the basis counting as excessively disjunctive. David Braddon-Mitchell drew my attention to a nice example here. Vitamins are a pretty heterogenous lot, but vitamin deficiency counts as a cause because there is a unity in the way lack of a vitamin acts on us. In the same way we should say that the reflectance triple story is one about how the possibly highly heterogeneous bases of the disposition to look red in different objects form a sufficiently unified disjunction to count as the normal cause of looking red.[23]

A nice feature of seeing the unity in causes as a matter of unity in the triples is that it squares with our allowing that the yellow-and-magenta-dotted look of an area of a colour magazine seen close up and its red-look seen from a normal viewing distance should *both* be thought of as revealing colour: one reveals the colour from close up, the other the colour from a normal viewing distance. For a triple of integrated reflectances is a holistic property of an area—an area as a whole may have a different triple value from that possessed by some sub-area. Thus, we can maintain that we are latching onto a physical property of the area when we view from a normal distance, and a different physical property of a sub-area of the larger area when we view from close up, because the categorical basis underlying the triple of integrated reflectances for an area will not in general be the same as that underlying the integrated triple of reflectances for a sub-area of the area.[24]

---

[23] I am much indebted here to comments by David Lewis, David Braddon-Mitchell, and Ian Gold on earlier fumblings with this point.

[24] Essentially the same account applies to the difference between blood seen

It is, however, unlikely that these possibly disjunctive bases will reflect the similarities and differences among the colours in the way that Hilbert's identifications arguably do. There is no reason to think the physical property we are latching onto when some particular thing looks red is similar to that we are latching onto when some particular thing looks pink, for example. This looks like trouble. For it is plausible that colour experience, in addition to representing objects as having properties which are causally responsible for these objects looking coloured, also represents these properties as occupying certain places in the three-dimensional colour array (red is opposite green, orange is nearer red than green, etc.). I think, though, that we need to ask: In what sense does, for instance, looking red represent objects as having a property more like the property looking orange represents them as having than does looking green; in what sense is orange as represented in experience more like red as represented in experience than it is like green as represented in experience?

A clearly wrong answer would be to say that it is somehow 'more' true or more obvious that orange is a different colour from green than that it is a different colour from red. It is certainly true and completely obvious *both* that red is different from orange and that red is different from green. The only alternative seems to be to borrow, in one form or another, from behavioural psychology by analysing the needed sense in terms of *jnds* (just noticeable differences). Roughly, the sense in which orange is closer to red than it is to green lies in the fact that it takes more jnds to get from orange of a given saturation to green of the same saturation than to get to red of the same saturation. But in *that* sense, or anything roughly like it, the physical properties do stand in the right similarity relationships. They induce the relevant behavioural relationships. More generally, the point is that if we can, as seems plausible, understand the three-dimensional array, the colour solid, in terms of suitably scaled jnds, then the nature of the array will not be trouble for the primary quality view.

However, none of this means that I can duck the question of what to say if it turns out that although there are some underlying

with the naked eye and blood seen through a microscope. See Hilbert, 'What is Color Vision?'.

unities among the objects that typically look red—it would be in-credible if there weren't—there is no single principle unifying them. The reflectance triples story, let us say, turns out to have major holes. Perhaps the red-looking objects naturally divide into two groups: in one group the categorical basis for looking red in the right way is one kind of structure S_1, and for the other it is some quite different structure S_2, and there is no way, in terms of reflectance triples or whatever, of seeing any sort of unity here.

In thinking about this case we should remember the example of jade. Jade, it turned out, comes in two quite different forms (nephrite and jadeite), but this did not lead us to deny the exist-ence of jade. It led us to say there are two kinds where we might have thought that there was only one. Likewise, if it turns out that there is no way of treating what makes tomatoes look red and what makes sunsets look red as different manifestations of some disjunctive but not excessively disjunctive common feature, we should say that the red of sunsets is a different property from the red of tomatoes just as New Zealand jade is a different kind from Chinese jade (though the two reds will occupy the same spot in the colour solid, of course). We should, that is, modify the axioms of unity. Redness is not the property in common to red things. Rather there are two rednesses, and red things have one or other of the two rednesses. I think that the folk would happily say this, and so that folk theory implicitly allows us to modify the axioms of unity. Indeed, I think that we could live with considerably more than two rednesses. What would be intolerable would be if it turns out that there are no interesting distinctive distal commonalities underlying similarities of apparent colour. For then what would be called for is not some more or less radical modification of the axioms of unity, but a total abandonment of them. If this turned out to be the case, I think that we would have to declare colour a pervasive illu-sion. Nothing is coloured, just as nothing has impetus in the sense given to it in medieval physics. Certain things appear to have impetus, which is how medieval physics made its mistake, but nothing really has it. We would have to say the same for colour.

The next two chapters are concerned with the location problem for ethics.

CHAPTER 5

The Location Problem for Ethics:
Moral Properties and Moral Content

IN this chapter and the next, I offer a solution to the location problem for ethics. I offer an account of how the ethical gets a place in the descriptive picture of what our world is like. By the descriptive picture, I mean the picture tellable in the terms that belong to the 'is' side of the famous 'is–ought' debate. By the time I have finished, you will have before you a schematic account of the meaning of ethical ascriptions and sentences in purely descriptive terms. In other words, I will be defending a version of what is often called definitional or analytical naturalism. However, I will call the doctrine analytical *descriptivism*. I want to avoid possible confusion with the separate question of how to find a place for the ethical in the picture of our world tellable in the terms of the natural or physical sciences. I do, though, briefly address the connection between descriptivism in ethics and a physicalist or naturalist metaphysics as the argument proceeds.

My discussion in these two chapters will be largely conducted under the assumption of *cognitivism*, and I start by saying something about this assumption.

COGNITIVISM

What it Is

Cognitivism, as I will understand it, is the doctrine that ethical sentences are truth-apt, where to be truth-apt is to be semantically able to have a truth-value. Sentences that are semantically able to have a truth-value typically have a truth-value, but there are exceptions. For example, when *A* is neither determinately pink nor determinately red, 'A is pink' is neither true nor false, but the sentence is truth-apt by virtue of the fact that its meaning does not debar it from having a truth-value—had A been appropriately different, the sentence would have had a truth-value. As R. M. Hare reminded me, the term 'cognitivism' is in some ways unfortunate; it wrongly suggests that those who deny truth-aptness, the noncognitivists, cannot, by definition, give the cognitive a role in ethical deliberation. Also, cognitivism in our sense is compatible with an extreme subjectivism according to which 'X is good' said by S is true iff S's immediate reaction to X is one of approval; for, on this view, although rational deliberation has no role to play in settling what is good, the sentence 'X is good' is truth-apt.

What does it take for a sentence to be truth-apt? Although we produce sentences for many reasons—to set off alarms, test out sound systems, and try out a new pen—we most especially use them to tell others, and our later selves, how things are. As we argued in Chapter 3, language is most especially a conventional system of physical structures for the communication of information, as Locke said, and as travellers in a foreign country whose language they do not understand are forcibly reminded when they get lost or try to buy something in a shop.[1] But to convey information is to make a division among the possibilities into those that are, and those that are not, in accord with how things are said to be. The truth-apt sentences, then, are those that, by virtue of the way they are used by speakers and writers, make a division among the possibilities into those that are in accord with how they represent things as being, and those that are not in accord with how they represent things as being; and the sentences are true just when things are as they represent them as being. (Or, at least, this is the kind of story to tell when the sentences are contingent, and the sentences we will be concerned with are contingent.)

---

[1] John Locke, *An Essay concerning Human Understanding*, Book III. Locke sometimes expresses matters in a way which invites the thought (and the consequent bad press) that he holds that words are really always about 'ideas'. But read aright, all he is saying is that the information we seek to disseminate is the information we take it we have to hand. I use the sentence 'The bus leaves at six' to disseminate the information that it leaves at six when I believe that it leaves at six. This does not mean that the sentence is about my belief that it does: both words and belief are about the bus and when it leaves.

Truth-Aptness and Disciplined Syntacticism

An obvious question is how this conception relates to a view on truth-aptness we might call *disciplined syntacticism*, recently canvassed by Crispin Wright, Paul Boghossian, and Paul Horwich.[2] On this view, a sentence is truth-apt if (a) it has the syntactical marks of truth-aptness—it permits the appending of the truth predicate, it may be properly embedded in belief contexts, it may figure in the antecedents and consequents of conditionals, it figures in logical inferences, is in the indicative mood, and the like, and (b) it is disciplined in the sense that there are clear standards governing when it is correct and when it is incorrect to use it: it is meaningful. It may (*may*) be that every sentence which passes these two tests is truth-apt in our sense, but we should not think of disciplined syntacticism as telling us what it *is* to be truth-apt. For satisfying the syntactic marks clause is not plausibly necessary for truth-aptness. There is no special reason why rather primitive languages that lack one or more of, say, the truth predicate, the indicative mood, and conditional constructions, cannot contain sentences that serve to represent how things are, thereby counting as truth-apt. At best, being disciplined and satisfying the syntactic marks of truth-aptness is one way of getting to represent how things are and, hence, of being truth-apt. Moreover, it is an open question whether or not being meaningful and 'syntactically right for truth' is sufficient for being truth-apt, even setting aside the hard issues raised by liar sentences and the like. For how a sentence represents things as being is an a posteriori, contingent matter.[3] It is a matter of the thoughts about how things are that the words and sentences, under the contingently adopted conventions of the language, are used to express. Roughly, 'pretty' stands for being pretty in English because the conventions of English imply

[2] Paul Boghossian, 'The Status of Content', *Philosophical Review*, 99 (1990): 157–84; Paul Horwich, 'Gibbard's Theory of Norms', *Philosophy and Public Affairs*, 22 (1993): 67–78; and Crispin Wright, *Truth and Objectivity* (Cambridge, Mass.: Harvard University Press, 1992) (from whom I take the term 'truth-apt'). As I read them, the canvassing is outright advocacy in Horwich but falls somewhat short of this in Wright and Boghossian.

[3] It may not be contingent and a posteriori how some sentence in English represents things as being in *English*, for it may be that we individuate languages in part by their representational properties. What is, then, contingent and a posteriori is that we, or anyone, speak English.

that the word 'pretty' is a word to use to tell English speakers that you take something to be pretty. Equally, 'jolie' stands for being pretty in French, because 'jolie' is a word to use in French to say that you take something to be pretty.

This means that it is an open possibility that some class of meaningful, declarative sentences fails to have the connection with taking things to be thus and so needed in order to count as representing that things are thus and so. This is exactly what many hold concerning indicative conditionals.[4] They ask: How should we settle how 'If *P* then *Q*' represents things as being? And answer, By reference to when competent speakers produce it when seeking to express how they take things to be. But competent speakers produce 'If *P* then *Q*' just when the conditional credence of *Q* given *P* is high enough in the circumstances for assertion. But, those who insist that indicative conditionals are not truth-apt go on to observe, the conditional credence of *Q* given *P* is not the credence of anything; it is, rather, a quotient of credences.[5] Hence, they conclude, there is no answer as to how indicative conditionals represent matters; there is no way things might be such that we produce 'If *P* then *Q*' when we give this way things might be sufficient credence, and so no way things might be that constitutes the condition under which 'If *P* then *Q*' is true.[6]

[4] The argument that follows can be found, in one form or another, in many places. See e.g. Ernest Adams, *The Logic of Conditionals* (Dordrecht: Reidel, 1975), and Dorothy Edgington, 'Do Conditionals have Truth Conditions?', in Frank Jackson, ed., *Conditionals* (Oxford: Oxford University Press, 1991), 176–201.

[5] This point received a major fillip from various proofs, following on in one way or another from David Lewis, 'Probabilities of Conditionals and Conditional Probabilities', *Philosophical Review*, 85 (1976): 297–315, that there is no *X* for which 'Pr(*Q* given *P*) = Pr(*X*)' holds with suitable generality. Ironically, Lewis himself holds that indicative conditionals have truth-conditions, and, in particular, those of the material conditional, as do I.

How then do I reply to argument given above? By arguing that although indicative conditionals do not have the standard connection with thought—the connection which would mean that you should assert them when you think that how they represents matters is likely enough for assertion—they have a connection close enough to the standard to confer truth-aptness (see my *Conditionals*, Oxford: Basil Blackwell, 1987, § 2. 6). Of course, closeness is a matter of degree, and it is vague how close is close enough to count as conferring truth-aptness. Consequently, a position on indicative conditionals well worth identifying is that it is indeterminate whether or not they have truth-conditions.

[6] Some have objected in discussion that we can give the conditions under which, say, 'If it rains then the match will be cancelled' is true; we simply write down

It is only under the assumption of cognitivism that ethics presents a location problem. If the non-cognitivists are right and ethical sentences do not represent things as being a certain way, there is no question of how to locate the way they represent things as being in relation to how accounts told in other terms—descriptive, physical, social or whatever—represent things as being, though there will still, of course, be a need to give an account of the meaning of ethical sentences and of what we are doing when we make ethical judgements (where, of course, to make an ethical judgement better not be literally to take things to be some way or other).

This chapter and the next are principally addressed to the conditional question, If I am to be a cognitivist, what sort should I be? Some non-cognitivists—an example is Simon Blackburn—regard the answer I will be giving to this question as *another* good reason for not being a cognitivist. As I understand his position, he is sympathetic to what I say cognitivists ought to hold, but regards it as providing an argument by *modus tollens* for not being a cognitivist. I, naturally, hope that the version of analytical descriptivism I will argue is the only viable position for the ethical cognitivist will be found sufficiently attractive in its own right to provide a reason in itself for being a cognitivist. Also, as we will observe in the next chapter, our arguments undercut some of the best-known arguments for non-cognitivism. So, although I cannot rule out non-cognitivism simply by noting that ethical sentences are meaningful and syntactically right for truth, I do think that it is very much a 'last resort' position.

I start by arguing that cognitivists must hold that ethical properties are descriptive properties.

ETHICAL PROPERTIES ARE DESCRIPTIVE PROPERTIES

The Role of Folk Theory

For cognitivists, terms like 'right', 'bad', 'immoral', and so on, are words for making claims about how things are. There are, that is,

'If it rains then the match will be cancelled' is true iff if it rains then the match will be cancelled.

This is grammatically fine, but the issue is not about grammar.

ethical and normative properties, including rightness, badness, and so on, provided we think of properties in the way described in Chapter 1. We are not taking a stand on the debates over universals in analytic ontology, but merely affirming that truth supervenes on being, and that successful predication supervenes on nature. Accordingly, the identification of rightness, for example, is a matter of identifying what is being claimed about how things are when it is said that some action is right. This means that if Tom tells us that what *he* means by a right action is one in accord with God's will, rightness according to Tom is being in accord with God's will. If Jack tells us that what *he* means by a right action is maximizing expected value as measured in hedons, then, for Jack, rightness is maximizing expected value. As Lewis Carroll said through the character of Humpty Dumpty, we are entitled to mean what we like by our words.[7] But if we wish to address the concerns of our fellows when we discuss the matter—and if we don't, we will not have much of an audience—we had better mean what they mean. We had better, that is, identify our subject via the *folk* theory of rightness, wrongness, goodness, badness, and so on. We need to identify rightness as the property that satisfies, or near enough satisfies, the folk theory of rightness—and likewise for the other moral properties. It is, thus, folk theory that will be our guide in identifying rightness, goodness, and so on.[8] Perhaps we will end up agreeing with Tom or Jack, but that should be the end of the story, not the beginning.

The Supervenience of the Ethical on the Descriptive

The most salient and least controversial part of folk moral theory is that moral properties supervene on descriptive properties, that the ethical way things are supervenes on the descriptive way things are.[9] I will start by arguing that the nature of the supervenience of

---

[7] Lewis Carroll, *Through the Looking Glass and What Alice Saw There*, see e.g. *The Annotated Alice*, ed. Martin Gardner (Harmondsworth: Penguin, 1965), 269. See also A. J. Ayer, *Language, Truth and Logic* (London: Gollancz, 1962), 105.

[8] Here I am rehearsing points made in a more general context in Chapter 2 under the heading 'Defining the Subject'.

[9] Or, rather, that is how to state the least controversial part of folk theory assuming cognitivism. Non-cognitivists insist, of course, that supervenience must be

the ethical on the descriptive tells us that ethical properties are descriptive properties in the sense of properties ascribed by language that falls on the descriptive side of the famous is–ought divide.[10]

The supervenience of the ethical on the descriptive is sometimes stated in an *intra*-world supervenience thesis: for all w, if x and y are descriptively exactly alike in w, they are ethically exactly alike in w. However, it is the global supervenience of the ethical on the descriptive that is important for us here. For we are concerned with how the descriptive nature of complete ways things might be settles ethical nature; and it is global supervenience theses that give us a handle on this question, precisely because they quantify over complete ways things might be.

We noted in Chapter 1 that it is a restricted, contingent, a posteriori global supervenience thesis that was called for to capture the sense in which it is at all plausible that the psychological globally supervenes on the physical. A global supervenience thesis like

> For all w and w^*, if w and w^* are exactly alike physically, then w and w^* are exactly alike psychologically

is non-controversially false.[11] The most that is plausible is that for any world physically exactly like our world, and which satisfies a certain additional constraint, roughly, a 'no gratuitous extras' constraint, is psychologically exactly like ours. However, the global supervenience of the ethical on the descriptive is special in that an unrestricted form, namely

> (S) For all w and w^*, if w and w^* are exactly alike descriptively then they are exactly alike ethically.

is both a priori true and necessary.

---

stated as some kind of constraint on those prescriptions, expressions of attitude, and the like, that count as moral judgements in their scheme.

[10] Ascribed, not denoted: 'the property we are mainly discussing' would typically count as descriptive, but it would be far too quick to infer from the fact that being right is the property denoted by 'the property we are mainly discussing' that it is descriptive.

[11] By the standards that apply in philosophy. There is a minority physicalist view on which this global supervenience thesis is true. On this view, it is a necessary a posteriori truth that each and every psychological state is a physical state. Nonphysical, thinking 'angels' embodied in 'ectoplasm' but having, say, all the 'right' functional roles occupied, are metaphysically impossible, and the intuition to the contrary arises from the fact that it is not a priori false that there are such angels.

Thesis (S) is compatible with the idea that ethical nature, the ethical way things are, is in part determined by facts about our responses and attitudes, with the appealing idea that, in Mark Johnston's terminology, value is response-dependent. For included in the global descriptive supervenience base will be facts about our responses, both actual and hypothetical, and both first- and higher-order, as described in purely descriptive terms (as wanting a glass of milk, say, and not as wanting something good).[12]

A fair question is how precisely to identify the purely descriptive terms. All I said earlier was that I meant what people have in mind by the 'is' side of the is–ought divide, or that they have in mind when they speak of factual or descriptive vocabulary, and factual and descriptive properties. My experience is that people either find the notion under any of its various names relatively unproblematic, in which case further explanation is unnecessary, or else no amount of explanation is of any use. But perhaps the following remarks will make matters clearer. Because I will be defending a descriptive analysis of ethical terms, I cannot hold that there is a sharp *semantic* divide between ethical and descriptive terms. I have to regard the purely descriptive terms as essentially given by a big list of terms that would generally be classified as such, and see the aim of the exercise as the analysis of ethical terms in some way or another in terms of this big list. Moreover, I need not assume that there is a sharp divide between descriptive and ethical vocabulary, any more than there is between being bald and not being bald. I can allow that it is vague whether the word 'honest', for example, should be classed as purely descriptive or as partly normative. For our purposes here, we can follow a play-safe strategy. If it is unclear whether a term is or is not purely descriptive, then we can take it off the list of the purely descriptive. For the supervenience thesis (S), on which the argument to follow turns, is plausible even after culling the terms about which there might reasonably be controversy as to their purely descriptive

---

12 Michael Smith, *The Moral Problem* (Oxford: Basil Blackwell, 1994), gives a special place to certain hypothetical desires, whereas David Lewis, 'Dispositional Theories of Value', *Proceedings of the Aristotelian Society*, supp. vol. 63 (1989): 113–37, gives a special place to certain second-order desires. For Mark Johnston on the response-dependent nature of value see e.g. 'Dispositional Theories of Value', *Proceedings of the Aristotelian Society*, supp. vol. 63 (1989): 139–74.

status. Finally, even if you belong to the party that thinks that the division between ethical and descriptive vocabulary is a hopeless confusion, and that the culling operation I just described could not be carried out in any principled way, there is still a question of interest in this area. We can ask, for any two lists of terms, with one designated 'descriptive' and the other 'ethical', independently of whether these labels are happy labels and of how we assigned the various terms to the two lists, whether or not (S) is true relative to the two lists.

Approaching the notion of a descriptive property in this way enables us to address a famous problem about what G. E. Moore means, or should mean, when he says that goodness is a *non-natural* property.[13] He does not mean that (moral) goodness is an ethical property; everyone who thinks that goodness is a property thinks that, and he is saying something intended to *differentiate* his view from that of many who hold that goodness is a property. He does not mean that goodness is not a property of happenings in the space-time world; it is a central part of his view that goodness is a property of such happenings. He does not mean that goodness is not the kind of property that figures in the physical sciences. It is clear that his arguments are as much directed to dualists as to physicalists: when he argues that goodness is not pleasure, his case does not rest on physicalism about pleasant sensations.[14] What he really wants to insist on, I think, is an *inadequacy* claim: what is left of language after we cull the ethical terms is in principle inadequate to the task of ascribing the properties we ascribe using the ethical terms. He wants to object to exactly the claim I will be making.

We noted in Chapter 1 that the restricted, contingent, a posteriori global supervenience of the psychological on the physical implies that the full physical account of our world entails the full psychological account of our world.[15] But the full psychological

---

[13] For Moore's worries about what he means, see 'A Reply to My Critics', in P. A. Schilpp, ed., *The Philosophy of G. E. Moore* (Chicago, Ill.: Northwestern University Press, 1942), 533–677, esp. 581–92.

[14] G. E. Moore, *Principia Ethica* (Cambridge: Cambridge University Press, 1929), 9.

[15] Remembering, first, that the entailment in question is spelt out in terms of necessary truth preservation, not a priori deduction (though I argued in Chapter 3 that the two-dimensional account of the necessary a posteriori yields the further

account does not entail the full physical account—no psychological account of our world, no matter how rich, entails each and every detail about where all the electrons are; and nor, on most views, does any and every psychological account of how things are entail some physical account of how things are—psychology might be realized in non-physical stuff.[16] There is, thus, no logical equivalence in general between the physical and psychological way things are. However, because of the special nature of the global supervenience of the ethical on the natural, there is a familiar argument (though I do not know who first advanced it) that shows that (S) has the consequence that any claim about how things are ethically is equivalent to some claim about how things are frameable in purely descriptive terms.

Let E be a sentence about ethical nature in the following sense: (a) E is framed in ethical terms and descriptive terms; (b) every world at which E is true has some ethical nature; and (c) for all w and w^*, if E is true at w and false at w^*, then w and w^* differ ethically. Intuitively, the idea is that E counts as being about ethical nature by virtue of the fact that there must be some ethical nature for it to be true, together with the fact that the only way to change its truth-value is by changing ethical nature; the worlds must, that is, differ somehow in the distribution of ethical properties and relations.[17] Now each world at which E is true will have some descriptive nature: ethical nature without descriptive nature is impossible (an evil act, for example, must involve death or pain or . . .). And, for each such world, there will be a sentence containing only descriptive terms that gives that nature in full. Now let w_1, w_2, etc. be the worlds where E is true, and let D_1, D_2, etc. be purely descriptive sentences true at w_1, w_2, etc., respectively, which give the full descriptive nature of w_1, w_2, etc. Then the disjunction

conclusion that physicalists are committed to the possibility in principle of a priori deducing the psychological way things are from the physical way things are), and, secondly, that the full physical account includes the no gratuitous extras or stop clause.

[16] The exception is the minority version of physicalism mentioned earlier, according to which every psychological state is identical with some physical state as a matter of metaphysical necessity.

[17] We thus rule out a sentence like 'There have been at least one hundred evil acts or tea-drinking is common'. Some worlds at which this sentence has different truth-values differ only in how common tea-drinking is.

of D_1, D_2, etc., will also be a purely descriptive sentence, call it D. But then E entails and is entailed by D. For every world where E is true is a world where one or other of the D_i is true, so E entails D. Moreover, every world where one or other of the D_i are true is a world where E is true, as otherwise we would have a violation of (S): we would have descriptively exactly alike worlds differing in ethical nature. Therefore, D entails E. The same line of argument can be applied *mutatis mutandis* to ethical and descriptive predicates and open sentences: for any ethical predicate there is a purely descriptive one that is necessarily co-extensive with it.

It follows that ethical properties are descriptive properties. For it is a consequence of the way the ethical supervenes on the descriptive that any claim about how things are made in ethical vocabulary makes no distinctions among the possibilities that cannot in principle be made in purely descriptive vocabulary. The result is stronger than the one we obtained for the relation between the physical account of our world and the psychological account of our world under the assumption of physicalism in Chapter 1. Even if physicalism is true, psychological vocabulary marks distinctions among the possibilities that cannot be marked in physical vocabulary. There are similarities between our world on the physicalists' conception of what our world is like, and the world according to Descartes, that cannot be captured in physical terms; and, of course, the point is even more marked for worlds that are quite unlike ours—two worlds made of different brands of ectoplasm might have all sorts of psychological similarities that could not be captured in physical terms. By contrast, ethical ways of partitioning the possibilities make no distinctions that are not mirrored in descriptive ways of partitioning them.

To avoid misunderstanding, I should emphasize two points at this stage. First, although for every ethical sentence, there is some equivalent purely descriptive sentence, it does *not* follow that there is no asymmetry between the ethical and descriptive accounts of how things are. A rich account of descriptive nature highly constrains ethical nature, and the full account of descriptive nature constrains ethical nature without remainder. This follows from the supervenience of the ethical on the descriptive. But a rich account of ethical nature leaves open many very different possibilities concerning descriptive nature. Even the full story about the ethical nature of a world w—in the sense of a story such that any world at which it is true is ethically exactly like *w*—is consistent with indefinitely many different descriptive natures, concerning, say, how certain distant and ethically insignificant electrons are moving. The relation between ethical nature and descriptive nature is in this regard like that between tallness and individual heights: '*x* is tall' is logically equivalent to some sentence about individual heights, but it is a hugely (and infinitely) disjunctive sentence about individual heights that it is equivalent to. Facts about individual heights typically highly constrain facts about who is tall, but not conversely, as we observed in the first chapter.

Secondly, it does not follow from the equivalence between *E* and *D* that ethical vocabulary is dispensable in practice. The disjunctive descriptive story *D* that is equivalent to the ethical story *E* may be an infinite disjunction we need ethical terms to handle. Consider the infinity of ways of having one's hair distributed that can make up being bald.[18] You can impart the concept of baldness by exhibiting examples—perhaps by pointing to one or another of one's acquaintances, or holding up photographs—but you cannot capture the feature that we pick out with the word 'bald' solely in terms of the language of hair distribution. You have at some stage to say that to be bald is to be *like* these exemplars in the 'bald' way, hoping that one's hearers have latched onto the relevant similarity and can go on in the right way. All the same, it does not follow that baldness is anything more than the relevant infinite disjunction of hair distributions. Moreover, we do not gain the mastery of the term 'bald' that we manifestly have by magic: there must be a similarity among the hair distributions—not a relation to some further property (what baldness 'really' is)—that we finite beings latch onto.[19] Likewise, ethical language may be needed in practice to capture the similarities among the various descriptive ways that (S) tells us constitute ethical nature, but ethical properties are, nevertheless, possibly infinitely disjunctive descriptive properties—there is nothing more 'there' other than the relevant similarities among those descriptive ways. There is no 'extra' feature that the

[18] And the relations between your hair distribution and the hair distribution of others, but we can simplify and ignore the relational part of the story.

[19] The similarity may be made salient for us by the fact that it is that similarity which prompts, after suitable training, the word 'bald', or an equivalent, in our mouths. See the discussion of paradigm-based concept acquisition in Chapter 3.

ethical terms are fastening onto, and we could in principle say it all in descriptive language (counting talk of similarities, including similarities made salient through a relation to we who use the ethical terms, as descriptive, of course).

Many, but Simon Blackburn in particular, have properly demanded an explanation of the supervenience of the ethical on the descriptive.[20] The answer, it seems to me, is given by the a priori nature of the supervenience: it tells us that it is part of our very understanding of ethical vocabulary that we use it to mark distinctions among the descriptive ways things are. If someone asks: Why does baldness supervene on hair distribution? the answer is that the a priori nature of the supervenience tells us that the explanation is that 'bald' *is* a word for marking a distinction among kinds of hair distributions. I think we should say the same for the ethical vocabulary: it is an implicit part (if it were explicit, the matter would not be philosophically controversial) of our understanding of ethical terms and sentences that they serve to mark distinctions among the descriptive ways things are.

The Objection from the Possibility of Logically Equivalent Predicates Picking Out Distinct Properties

I now digress to consider an objection that turns on the possibility of logically equivalent predicates picking out different properties. As we noted in Chapter 1, some hold that the property of being an equilateral triangle and the property of being an equiangular triangle are distinct properties, despite the logical equivalence of '*x* is an equiangular triangle' and '*x* is an equilateral triangle'. They argue, for example, from the fact that we can think that a triangle is equilateral but fail to think that it is equiangular that they are distinct properties. Thus, it might be objected that the equivalence of the ethical and descriptive sentences and terms we derived from (S) leaves open the possibility that ethical properties and descriptive properties are related in something like the way that being an equiangular triangle and being an equilateral one are: they are necessarily co-extensive but distinct all the same.

---

[20] See e.g. Simon Blackburn, 'Supervenience Revisited', in Ian Hacking, ed., *Exercises in Analysis: Essays by Students of Casimir Lewy* (Cambridge: Cambridge University Press, 1985).

However, on the conception of property we are working with—the conception of a way things might be, an aspect of the world, not an aspect of our discourse or thought about it—we should insist that we have here one property and not two. Cases where we think that a triangle is equiangular while failing to think that it is equilateral are ones where we have a separation in modes of representation in thought for what is, all the same, one and the same property in our sense of 'property'. We have two ways of singling out or representing to ourselves what is one and the same potential feature of reality.

A different argument sometimes offered for distinguishing being an equilateral triangle from being an equiangular one is that we could design a machine to detect whether something is an equilateral triangle without designing it to detect whether it is an equiangular one. And in such a case could not, it is argued, the flashing of a light on the machine be causally explained by an object's being an equilateral triangle but not by its being an equiangular triangle?[21] Here, it seems, we have reason to make a distinction *in re* between being an equilateral triangle and being an equiangular one, not just a distinction between our ways of representing how things are *in re*, for we have a difference in explanatory role with respect to what happens.

However, when we consider the detail of how such a machine might operate, the force of the example evaporates. The machine, we may suppose, takes triangles and in turn measures their sides, determines whether they are all equal, and if they are, trips a circuit that leads to the light's flashing. It is plausible in this kind of case that a triangle's being equilateral explains the light's flashing, but the triangle's being equiangular does not. After all, the machine never even gets to measure the angles, so how could the angles' all being equal be what does the explaining? But the force of the example derives from the fact that we have a segmented process, one part of which especially involves the sides rather than the angles. The reason it is correct, or anyway more intuitive, to explain the light's flashing in terms of the triangle's being equi-

---

[21] The example is a variant on one discussed in Elliott Sober, 'Why Logically Equivalent Properties May Pick Out Different Properties', *American Philosophical Quarterly*, 19 (1982): 183–90. I am indebted in my discussion here to David Braddon-Mitchell.

lateral is that sides play a causal role along the way to the light's flashing that angles do not. But this only bears on the common ground doctrine that sides are distinct from angles. It is irrelevant to the issue about whether being an equilateral triangle is distinct from being an equiangular triangle.

This argument is essentially negative. I have explained why I find a certain alleged example of distinct but necessarily co-extensive properties unconvincing. Let me now add some positive considerations against holding that ethical properties are distinct from, though necessarily co-extensive with, descriptive properties.

First, it is hard to see how we could ever be justified in interpreting a language user's use of, say, 'right' as picking out a property distinct from that which the relevant purely descriptive predicates pick out, for we know that the complete story about how and when the language user produces the word 'right' can be given descriptively.

Secondly, it is hard to see how the further properties could be of any ethical significance. Are we supposed to take seriously someone who says, 'I see that this action will kill many and save no-one, but that is not enough to justify my not doing it; what really matters is that the action has an extra property that only ethical terms are suited to pick out'? In short, the extra properties would ethical 'idlers'.

And, finally, we can distinguish a more and a less extreme view. The extreme view says that for every (contingent) descriptive way there is, there is a quite distinct, necessarily co-extensive non-descriptive—ethical as it might be—way there is. This extreme version is hard to take seriously. It seems an absurdly anti-Occamist multiplication of properties: for *every* descriptive property, we have a corresponding non-descriptive one! But if the idea is that the duplication only happens occasionally, where is the principled basis for saying when it happens and when it does not?[22] What is special about the descriptive properties that have twins from those that do not? It is hard to give a non-arbitrary answer to this question. What is more, it is hard to see how we could be assured that the twinning occurs when and only when we use ethical terms.

---

[22] I owe this point to David Lewis.

Even if twinning does sometimes occur, how could we be confident that our use of ethical language coincides with those occasions?

Arguing from Supervenience versus Arguing from Metaphysical Fantasy

It might be wondered why I bother to argue from the supervenience thesis, (S), to the conclusion that cognitivists must identify ethical properties with descriptive ones. Can't we reject Moore's style of cognitivism as a metaphysical fantasy, as Allan Gibbard, A. J. Ayer, and Gilbert Harman, for instance, do?[23] However, what is plausible as a thesis in metaphysics concerns the kinds of properties that are *instantiated*. It is plausible that the kinds of things we morally evaluate lack any non-natural properties in Moore's sense: given what we know about what our world is like, it is hard to believe that there are instantiated properties that, as a matter of principle, cannot be ascribed by descriptive language. Indeed, many will go further and insist if ethical properties are to be instantiated, we had better identify them with *physical* properties.[24] *Realists*—that is, cognitivists who take the extra step of holding that the ethical properties are instantiated, that the relevant truth-apt sentences are on occasion true—cannot identify ethical properties with Moorean non-natural properties. The importance of the argument from supervenience is that it shows that cognitivists should identify ethical properties with descriptive ones independently of their metaphysical views about what things are like, and, in particular, independently of whether they hold that the ethical properties are in fact possessed by anything.

This means that there is a further important difference between the supervenience of the psychological on the physical and the supervenience of the ethical on the descriptive. You could have no good reason to accept the supervenience of the psychological on the physical unless you held certain metaphysical views. The supervenience of the ethical on the descriptive is, by contrast, *prior* to metaphysics. It tells us what the possibilities are for the kinds of

---

[23] A. J. Ayer, 'On the Analysis of Moral Judgements', repr. in *Philosophical Essays* (London: Macmillan, 1959), 231–49, see 235; Allan Gibbard, *Wise Choices: Apt Feelings* (Cambridge, Mass.: Harvard University Press, 1990); and Gilbert Harman, *The Nature of Morality* (New York: Oxford University Press, 1977).

[24] See e.g. Gibbard, *Wise Choices: Apt Feelings*, 123.

properties ethical properties might be—for, that is, the kinds of ways things might be marked out by ethical language—and leaves it as a further question whether the properties in question are in fact instantiated.

WHICH DESCRIPTIVE PROPERTIES ARE WHICH ETHICAL PROPERTIES?

The supervenience of the ethical on the descriptive gives cognitivists strong reason to identify ethical properties with descriptive properties, but is silent on *which* descriptive property each ethical property is. I now describe and defend a general method for pairing off ethical and descriptive properties, without actually doing the pairing off. We will see why the job cannot, as of now, be completed. Which descriptive properties are which ethical properties depends on matters that remain to be settled.

Moral Functionalism

I said, following Humpty Dumpty, that we can mean what we like by our words. But if we want to speak to the concerns of our fellows, we had better mean by our words what they mean. If we are interested in which property the word 'right' in the mouths of the folk picks out, we had better give a central place to folk opinion on the subject. We have already appealed to one central part of folk opinion in using the supervenience of the ethical on the descriptive to argue that ethical properties are descriptive properties. Moral functionalism continues the policy by letting the totality of folk opinion settle which descriptive properties are which ethical properties, though we will see later that this is compatible with letting some parts of folk opinion play a privileged role. Philip Pettit and I use the term 'moral functionalism' for this theory in order to highlight the parallel with the familiar story told by common-sense or analytical functionalism in the philosophy of mind about how mental state terms pick out the, as it happens, neurophysiological states that they do pick out.[25]

---

[25] The account that follows is indebted to John (I. G.) Campbell and Robert

In the case of the mind, we have a network of interconnected and interdefinable concepts that get their identity through their place in the network. We do not understand them one by one but, rather, holistically through their location in the network. The network itself is the theory known as folk psychology, a theory we have a partly tacit and a partly explicit grasp of. The explicit bits are the parts we can write down more or less straight off the bat. The implicit bits are the parts that it takes reflection on possible cases to tease out of us. Those good enough at theory construction could extract and articulate the patterns that guide us in classifying the various possible cases, but we cannot do the job, or anyway cannot as of now do the job. Our mastery of grammar is often used to illustrate the central idea. We have a folk theory of grammar with some clauses we can write down more or less roughly—'Verbs should agree with subjects', for example—but there is a lot that only expert grammarians can write down, despite the fact that what they write down is based on what we folk do when we classify a sentence as grammatical: they take *our* classifications and seek to articulate what is guiding us in making those classifications. This part of the story, together with the part that the grammarians have yet to write down, is the implicit part.

In the case of ethics, we have *folk morality*: the network of moral opinions, intuitions, principles and concepts whose mastery is part and parcel of having a sense of what is right and wrong, and of being able to engage in meaningful debate about what ought to be done. We can think of it as being like folk psychology in having a tripartite nature: like folk psychology, it contains input clauses, internal role clauses, and output clauses. The input clauses of folk morality tell us what kinds of situations described in descriptive, non-moral terms warrant what kinds of description in ethical terms: if an act is an intentional killing, then normally it is wrong; pain is bad; 'I cut, you choose' is a fair procedure; and so on. The internal role clauses of folk morality articulate the interconnections between matters described in ethical, normative language: courageous people are more likely to do what is right than cowardly people; the best option is the right option; rights impose

Pargetter, 'Goodness and Fragility', *American Philosophical Quarterly*, 23 (1986): 155–66, and Lewis, 'Dispositional Theories of Value', in spirit if not in letter.

duties of respect; and so on. The output clauses of folk morality
take us from ethical judgements to facts about motivation and thus
behaviour: the judgement that an act is right is normally accompanied by at least some desire to perform the act in question; the realization that an act would be dishonest typically dissuades an
agent from performing it; properties that make something good
are the properties we typically have some kind of pro-attitude towards, and so on. Moral functionalism, then, is the view that the
meanings of the moral terms are given by their place in this network of input, output, and internal clauses that makes up folk
morality.[26]

Although moral functionalism gets its name because of the parallel with common-sense functionalism in the philosophy of mind,
there are at least two important respects in which moral functionalism differs from common-sense functionalism. First, its principles are not causal principles. The principle that a fair division of
some good is, other things equal, morally better than an unfair division, does not say that being fair typically causes things to be
morally better. Again, the principle that acts that cause suffering
are typically wrong is not the principle that the suffering causes
the wrongness of the act. An act may be wrong because it causes
suffering, but the 'because' is not a causal one. (The act does not
become wrong a moment after it causes the suffering.) The principles of folk morality tell us which properties typically go together, but not by virtue of causing each other.

Secondly, the principles of folk morality are more controversial
than the principles of common-sense functionalism—a point that
calls for a little discussion.

The principles of folk morality are what we appeal to when we
debate moral questions. They are the tenets we regard as settling
our moral debates: 'All right, you've convinced me. It would be a
betrayal of friendship not to testify on Jones's behalf, so I'll testify.'
The appearance of phrases like this marks that some tenet—in this

[26] There is a distinction between giving the meaning and fixing the reference familiar from Kripke, *Naming and Necessity*. My phrasing may suggest that moral
functionalism is wedded to a term's place in the network giving the meaning in
Kripke's sense. In fact, however, I take moral functionalism to be neutral on
whether place in the network gives the meaning in Kripke's sense or fixes the reference in Kripke's sense. This question is addressed further in the next chapter.

case, that it is wrong to betray friendship—is a part of our shared folk moral theory. However, this does not mean that it is unrevisable. The dispute settling nature of such a tenet shows that *at the time in question and relative to the audience with whom we are debating*, the tenet is part of our folk morality. If there were not such benchmarks in our discussions of moral questions, we could not hold a sensible moral discussion with our fellows. Nevertheless, these benchmark tenets are far from immutable, and are in fact in the process of being revised in the ongoing moral debate—as carried out in the newspapers, universities, between consenting adults, and so on and so forth. Folk morality is currently under negotiation: its basic principles, and even many of its derived ones, are a matter of debate and are evolving as we argue about what to do.

What is, though, true is that there is a considerable measure of agreement about the general principles *broadly stated*. We agree that, by and large, promises ought to be kept; we agree that killing people is normally wrong; we agree that people who claim to believe that something is very wrong but show not the slightest inclination to refrain from doing it are in some sense insincere; we agree that certain character traits associated with the virtues are intimately connected with persons' dispositions to do what is right; and so on. And if we did not share a good number of opinions of this sort, it is hard to see how we could be said to have a common moral language. Genuine moral disagreement, as opposed to mere talking past one another, requires a background of shared moral opinion to fix a common, or near enough common, set of meanings for our moral terms. We can think of the rather general principles that we share as the commonplaces or platitudes or constitutive principles that make up the core we need to share in order to count as speaking a common moral language. What we disagree about are the fundamental underpinnings of these generally agreed principles, and, accordingly, we disagree about the nature and frequency of the exceptions to them. For example, consequentialists and deontologists mostly agree that promises ought to be kept, that killing people is wrong, and that there are exceptions to both principles; but they disagree sharply about the nature and frequency of the exceptions. Again, most of us agree that informed consent is to be preferred to uninformed consent, but there is a great deal of disagreement about exactly why this is so.

This means that it is still very much up in the air where we will be after the dust has settled. We are currently seeking some kind of consensus about the nature and frequency of the exceptions to the general principles we share. If John Rawls's influential account is right, systematic moral thinking involves the attempt to balance compelling general principles against considered judgements about how various options should be characterized.[27] We can think of this story as one story about how folk morality should evolve over time: we modify folk morality under the constraint of reconciling the most compelling general principles with particular judgements. In this way we hope to end up with some kind of consensus.

In any case, however we should characterize the way folk morality is evolving over time, it is useful to have a term for where folk morality will end up after it has been exposed to debate and critical reflection (or would end up, should we keep at it consistently and not become extinct too soon). I will call where folk morality will end up, mature folk morality. The idea is that mature folk morality is the best we will do by way of making good sense of the raft of sometimes conflicting intuitions about particular cases and general principles that make up current folk morality. For example, we have, it seems to me, currently no clear sense of the place and rationale of the distinction between doing and allowing in folk morality. We appear to give it a central role when we distinguish sharply between the immorality of killing someone, and that of refraining from contributing to famine relief even when we know that a consequence of so doing is that someone will die. And yet it is notorious that it is very hard to say *why* the difference between doing and allowing should be so important in a way which squares with our intuitions about other cases and makes good general sense.[28] Perhaps we will resolve this clash by following the consequentialists and abandoning the moral significance of the distinction, and, as a result, increase markedly how much we

---

[27] John Rawls, *A Theory of Justice* (Oxford: Oxford University Press, 1971).

[28] See e.g. Shelly Kagan, *The Limits of Morality* (Oxford: Clarendon Press, 1989), and Jonathan Glover, *Causing Death and Saving Lives* (Harmondsworth: Penguin, 1977).

contribute to famine relief. Perhaps we will find the as-yet elusive clarification and vindication of the distinction between doing and allowing—or some other distinction, perhaps a version of that between direct and oblique intentions, that serves the same purpose of saving our intuition that it is much worse to kill than to fail to give to famine relief—which avoids forcing us into grossly counter-intuitive verdicts in other cases. At present the situation is unclear (though I will not conceal my opinion that the consequentialists are winning the debate).[29] What is important for us here is that the present situation is unstable, and thus serves as an example where mature folk morality will need to differ from current folk morality.

A second, much-discussed case is the debate over abortion and infanticide. Most of us take a very different attitude to abortion as opposed to infanticide: we allow that the first is permissible in many circumstances, but that the second is hardly ever permissible, and yet it is hard to justify this disparity in moral judgement in the sense of finding a relevant difference. Some think that we should abandon the disparity—by changing our attitude to infanticide, or our attitude to abortion. Most of us think that we should look harder for the relevant difference.

The Ecumenical Nature of Moral Functionalism

It is no part of moral functionalism that all parts of the network that is folk morality are equal. Although the view is that we should seek the best way of constructing a coherent theory out of folk morality, respecting as much as possible those parts that we find most appealing, to form mature folk morality, it may well be that one part or other of the network is fundamental in the sense that our search for mature folk morality will go best if we seek to derive the whole story starting at that part. The history of ethical theory is full of attempts to identify, out of the mass of moral opinions we find initially appealing, a relatively small number of fundamental insights from which all of what we find (or will or would find) most plausible under critical reflection—that is, what we have just agreed to call mature folk morality—can be derived.

---

[29] See e.g. Frank Jackson, 'Decision-Theoretic Consequentialism and the Nearest and Dearest Objection', *Ethics*, 101 (1991): 461–82.

Utilitarians, for example, argue that a simple connection between rightness and maximizing happiness delivers all the rest. They have to acknowledge that a certain amount of 'damage' occurs along the way. They can easily show that it is, as a rule, wrong to punish the innocent, but what makes it wrong is not quite what we thought when we started. The principle of folk morality that it is wrong to punish the innocent becomes a more contingent one, with more in the way of exceptions than is initially appealing. Utilitarians seek to convince us that critical reflection shows that the highly contingent principle that they deliver is all that we should seek—and so, to put the point in our terms, is all that we should want in mature folk morality. Likewise, contractarians, Kantians, ideal observer theorists, universal prescriptivists, virtue theorists, and so on, can all be seen as having special stories to tell that start from one or another part of what we find intuitively plausible—from, that is, one or another part of current folk morality. They then seek to recover enough of folk morality, or enough of a clearly recognizable descendant of folk morality that stands up to critical reflection, to form mature folk morality. And this, it seems, is how things must be. Folk morality is a highly complex system. It is to be expected that we should start with a fragment that particularly appeals to us and seek to reconstruct the rest, near enough, from that fragment. Moreover, we must start from somewhere in current folk morality, otherwise we start from somewhere *unintuitive*, and that can hardly be a good place to start from. And we must seek a theory that stands up to critical reflection: it can hardly be desirable to end up with a theory that fails to stand up to critical reflection.

I take it to be a major argument in favour of moral functionalism that the story we have just rehearsed (sketched) well describes what actually goes on when we debate views in ethics. We tease out the consequences of the view or views under discussion; we identify those that seem most at odds with current folk morality—in other words, the consequences which strike us as most counterintuitive; and consider whether we are prepared after critical reflection to accept the consequences, that is, to modify folk morality so as to accord with them.

Moral functionalism is also neutral on the issue between centralism and non-centralism in ethics. Centralism in ethics holds that the *central* or, as they are sometimes called, following Bernard

Williams, the *thin* ethical concepts—right, wrong, good, bad, ought, and ought not—are the conceptually fundamental ones. The various *thick* ethical concepts—courage, inequity, promising, and the like; that is, those that imply a distinctive descriptive nature in addition to an ethical dimension—can then be thought of conjunctively as the result of marrying some nature as capturable by the central ethical concepts with some purely descriptive nature.[30] By contrast, non-centralism, recently espoused by Susan Hurley, for example, insists that the thin ethical concepts are not fundamental.[31] Rightness, what one ought to do, goodness, and the like, are not conceptually prior to kindness, equity, and the like.

Moral functionalism can be given a centralist gloss or a non-centralist gloss. In its centralist gloss, it insists that a certain fragment of the network which contains no mention of the thick ethical concepts suffices to identify the thin ethical concepts. We can identify the thin ethical concepts by identifying their place in a network that makes no mention of equity, kindness, and the like. On this view, if we say enough about which naturalistically described situations merit which thin ethical descriptions, enough about the interconnections between situations described in thin ethical terms, and enough about the connection between judgements of thin ethical nature and facts about motivation, we will pin down the thin ethical concepts. By contrast, the non-centralist version of moral functionalism insists that we must include the parts of the network that concern matters described in thick ethical terms. Thus, it might be urged that it is part of a proper grasp of the concept of right action that we know that the cowardly are less likely to do what is right than the courageous, that it is sometimes right to be merciful, and the like. Indeed, it seems to me that moral functionalism is not only neutral as between centralism and non-centralism, it enables us to give sharp expression to what is at issue. Centralists are precisely those who hold, and non-centralists

---

[30] R. M. Hare defends centralism in many places, see e.g. *Freedom and Reason* (Oxford: Clarendon Press, 1963), ch. 10. For the thick–thin terminology, see Williams, *Ethics and the Limits of Philosophy*.

[31] Susan Hurley, *Natural Reasons: Personality and Polity* (New York: Oxford University Press, 1989).

those who deny, that we can make sense of the thin ethical concepts independently of the thick ones, and the network approach distinctive of moral functionalism tells us what that issue comes to: we can make sense of the thin ethical concepts independently of the thick ethical concepts if and only if the network minus the bits that contain thick ethical terms is sufficient to fix the meanings of the thin ethical terms.

I have spoken as if there will be, at the end of the day, some sort of convergence in moral opinion in the sense that mature folk morality will be a single network of input, output, and internal role clauses accepted by the community as a whole. In this case we can talk simply of mature folk morality without further qualification. Indeed, I take it that it is part of current folk morality that convergence will or would occur. We have some kind of commitment to the idea that moral disagreements can be resolved by sufficient critical reflection—which is why we bother to engage in moral debate. To that extent, some sort of objectivism is part of current folk morality.[32] But this may turn out to be, as a matter of fact, false. Indeed, some hold that we know enough as of now about moral disagreement to know that convergence will (would) not occur. In this case, there will not be a single mature folk morality but rather different mature folk moralities for different groups in the community; and, to the extent that they differ, the adherents of the different mature folk moralities will mean something different by the moral vocabulary because the moral terms of the adherents of the different schemes will be located in significantly different networks. I set this complication aside in what follows. I will assume what I hope and believe is the truth of the matter, namely, that there will (would) be convergence. But if this is a mistake, what I say in what follows should be read as having implicit relativization clauses built into it. The identifications of the ethical properties should all be read as accounts, not of rightness *simpliciter*, but of rightness for this, that, or the other moral community, where what defines a moral community is that it is a group of people who would converge on a single mature folk morality starting from current folk morality.

---

[32] On the central role of convergence, see Smith, *The Moral Problem*, § 6. 3.

CHAPTER 6

Analytical Descriptivism

IN the last chapter I argued that cognitivists in ethics should be descriptivists. The crucial argument was that the special nature of the famous supervenience of the ethical on the descriptive shows that any ethical way of carving up how things are is equivalent to some descriptive way of carving up how things are. This leaves open how to find the right descriptive account for any given ethical account of how things are, and I proceeded to outline a way of interconnecting the ethical and descriptive accounts of how things are. The key idea was to take folk morality, our present raft of intuitions about how descriptive and moral accounts of how things are interconnect, and consider what folk morality will (would) turn into in the limit under critical reflection—mature folk morality, as I called it—and then let mature folk morality make the interconnections for us.

It is hard to see how else we could approach the task: to start with something other than folk morality would be to follow the unattractive policy of starting somewhere unintuitive, and critical reflection is, by definition, what any theory should be subjected to. Of course, precisely what critical reflection on current folk morality comes to in detail is a matter of considerable debate, and I noted that the general picture I describe might be fleshed out in different ways by virtue theorists, consequentialists, deontologists, and so on. Equally, the story might be told in the terms favoured by R. M. Hare. In this case, the emphasis would be on whether or not one or another part of current folk morality survives the demand that we be prepared to universalize its prescriptions.[1]

I start the business of this chapter by showing how this method of interconnecting ethical and descriptive accounts enables us to identify each ethical property with some descriptive property. I

---

[1] See e.g. Hare, *Freedom and Reason*, ch. 6.

then contrast the descriptivism I am defending with 'Cornell realism', and proceed to discuss what our version of descriptivism should say about the open question argument, and about the direction problem (the sense in which moral judgement points towards or away from action).

IDENTIFYING THE ETHICAL PROPERTIES

Using Lewis on Theoretical Terms

We identify the ethical properties by applying the method of defining theoretical terms developed by David Lewis, drawing on work by F. P. Ramsey and Rudolf Carnap, to mature folk morality, the theory on which current folk morality will converge under critical reflection.[2]

Let **M** be mature folk morality. Imagine it written out as a long conjunction with the moral predicates written in property name style. For example, 'Killing someone is typically wrong' becomes 'Killing typically has the property of being wrong'. Replace each distinct moral property term by a distinct variable to give $M(x_1, x_2, \ldots)$. Then '$(\exists x_1) \ldots M(x_1, \ldots)$' is the Ramsey sentence of **M**, and

$$(\exists x_1) \ldots (y_1) \ldots (M(y_1, \ldots) \text{ iff } x_1 = y_1 \ \& \ x_2 = y_2 \ldots)$$

is the modified Ramsey sentence of **M** which says that there is a unique realization of **M**.

If moral functionalism is true, **M** and the modified Ramsey sentence of **M** say the same thing. For that is what holding that the ethical concepts are fixed by their place in the network of mature folk morality comes to.[3] Fairness is what fills the fairness role; rightness is what fills the rightness role; and so on. We can now say what it is for some action *A* to be, say, right, as follows:

(R) *A* is right iff $(\exists x_1) \ldots (A \text{ has } x_r \ \& \ (y_1) \ldots (M(y_1, \ldots) \text{ iff } x_1 = y_1 \ \& \ldots))$

---

[2] See Lewis, 'How to Define Theoretical Terms'.
[3] Or at least it is if it is part of folk theory that there is a unique realization. This assumption deserves further discussion.

where 'x_r' replaced 'being right' in **M**. We now have our account of when A is right: it is right just if it has the property that plays the rightness role as specified by the right-hand side of (R), a property we can be confident is a purely descriptive one, given the unrestricted, global, a priori supervenience of the ethical on the descriptive. Clearly, the same procedure, with appropriate modifications, will yield an account when A is good, just, fair, bad, and so on. For all the ethical predicates, thick or thin, we have an account of their truth- or application-conditions. What is more, we have an account in purely descriptive terms, because the modified Ramsey sentence is obtained by replacing *all* the ethical terms by bound variables.

This in itself does not tell us what rightness, the property, is, and the same goes for goodness, etc. It is a story about truth-conditions, but does not tell us about the metaphysics of rightness. In particular, it leaves open two possibilities: that rightness is the (first-order) descriptive, possibly disjunctive property that plays the rightness role, the realizer property as it is called in the corresponding debate in the philosophy of mind, or that it is the second-order property of having the property that plays the rightness role, the role property as it is called in the corresponding debate in the philosophy of mind.[4] However, there seems a clear reason for favouring the first view. We want rightness to be what makes an action right, not in the causal sense but in the sense of being what ought to be aimed at. Now what we should aim at is not doing what is right *qua* what is right. I should rescue someone from a fire because if I don't they will die, not because that is the right thing to do. True, being motivated by an act's being right is better than being motivated by the desire to get one's picture in the papers. All the same, what ought to motivate us, and what we should value and pursue, is not the moral status of our actions *per se,* but the goods that confer that moral status.[5] But from the perspective of moral functionalism, the choice between role property and realizer property is the choice between the moral property *per se*, and what makes something right in the sense of being the rightness part of the best solution to the equations of mature folk morality; that is, the property which is such that putting its name in place of 'x_r' in

---

[4] See e.g. Jackson and Pettit, 'Functionalism and Broad Content'.
[5] See e.g. Smith, *The Moral Problem*, 74–6.

'$(\exists x_1) \ldots (y_1) \ldots (M(y_1, \ldots)$ iff $x_1 = y_1$ & $x_2 = y_2 \ldots)$' makes it true. Or near enough true. We should not expect perfect solutions here any more than in physics where we found what the term 'atom' denoted by finding something that near enough satisfied atomic theory.[6] To illustrate with a controversial hypothesis, suppose it turns out that the best solution to the equations of mature folk morality, the solution that makes them true (near enough), includes 'x is right if and only if x maximizes expected hedonic value', and 'x is good if and only if x has positive expected hedonic value', then the claim is that we should identify rightness with maximizing expected hedonic value, and goodness with positive expected hedonic value, because they will then be *what* we value and ought to aim at.

This means that there is a second sense in which moral functionalism is ecumenical, and so is a *schema* for viewing what goes on when we seek a moral theory, rather than a substantive theory in itself. In the last chapter we focused on the point that moral functionalism can allow that different parts of the network are more or less fundamental, in the sense of being the part from which the rest can be derived when we seek mature folk morality. But if rightness, to stick with this example, should be viewed as the first-order property that occupies the rightness role, then we have two questions to ask of rightness: first, what is the essential feature or features of the rightness role, and, secondly, what property occupies the role so identified? And it may turn out, or at least it may turn out for all that moral functionalism says, that virtue theory, say, is the correct answer to the first question, whereas utilitarianism is the correct answer to the second question. That is, it may turn out that

(1) Rightness is the property distinctive of the acts of the virtuous,

and

(2) The property distinctive of the acts of the virtuous is maximizing expected utility,

---

[6] Alternatively, we might, as David Lewis pointed out to me, make it part of the maturing process to find an M such that '$(\exists x_1) \ldots (y_1) \ldots (M(y_1, \ldots)$ iff $x_1 = y_1$ & $x_2 = y_2 \ldots)$' is true *simpliciter*.

are *both* true. But (1) expresses a view about the rightness role, a view we can regard as a style of virtue theory, presumably advanced as an a priori truth of some kind; whereas (2) expresses an a posteriori view about the property that fills the rightness role as expressed in (1), and, when combined with (1), constitutes a style of utilitarianism. From the perspective of moral functionalism, virtue theory and utilitarianism are not by their very nature inconsistent.[7] Or consider the path Hare takes that leads him from universalizable prescriptivism to utilitarianism.[8] He starts, to say it in our terms, from a claim about the rightness role—roughly, that rightness is the property that we can universally prescribe—and ends, to say it in our terms, with the claim that the property which fills that role is maximizing expected utility, impartially considered.

I have now told the story about how to identify the ethical properties: find the properties which are such that, going under their purely descriptive property names, they make the clauses of mature folk morality come out true (near enough), and then identify each ethical property with the corresponding descriptive property. There is, however, an important further question, noted in passing in the previous chapter, to be addressed.

Rigidity

We can think of the specification of truth-conditions offered by moral functionalism in two different ways. We can think of it as giving the meaning of, say, 'right' in the traditional sense. An action is right in a possible world if and only if it has the property that fills the 'x_r' position in that world. In this case

(R) A is right iff $(\exists x_1) \ldots (A$ has x_r & $(y_1) \ldots (M(y_1, \ldots)$ iff $x_1 = y_1$ & $\ldots))$

is both a priori and necessary, and if we combine this with our claim about the right metaphysics for moral functionalism, the term 'rightness' will come out as a non-rigid definite description for the property that fills the rightness role, and, in consequence,

---

[7] I am indebted here to discussions with Philip Pettit and Michael Smith.
[8] See e.g. Hare, *Freedom and Reason*, ch. 7.

which property rightness is may vary from world to world. Alternatively, we can think of the specification of truth-conditions as fixing the reference of the term 'right'. An action is right in a possible world if and only if it has the property that fills the 'x_r' role in the *actual* world. In this case, (R) is a priori but not necessary, and if we combine this with our claim about the right metaphysics for moral functionalism, the terms for the moral properties will come out as rigidified definite descriptions or descriptive names, and rightness will be that which *actually* fills the rightness role. On this construal, rightness is the same property in all possible worlds.

I spoke of moral functionalism when I first introduced it as *giving the meaning* of the moral vocabulary, and this (as we noted in a footnote) suggests the first reading. I should, therefore, emphasize that moral functionalism here is to be read as silent on the question of rigidity versus non-rigidity. For what it is worth, it seems to me that current folk morality favours the rigid reading. But whether this will survive into mature folk morality I do not know. The issues of realism and direction to be addressed below are independent of the answer to this question—if indeed there is a such a thing as *the* answer, for, as David Lewis has convinced me, often the question of rigidity has no determinate answer.

ANALYTICAL DESCRIPTIVISM VERSUS ONTOLOGICAL DESCRIPTIVISM

The Contrast with Cornell Realism

I have been defending a view according to which the ethical properties are one and all descriptive properties. My version of this view, though, is different from the well-known version of this view that sometimes goes under the name of 'Cornell realism' (and is often called a version of naturalism, but, as explained in the previous chapter, I want to avoid any possible confusion with naturalism in the philosophy of mind). According to Cornell realism as I will understand it, (a) ethical properties are identical with descriptive properties, (b) the relevant statements of the identities are necessary a posteriori, and (c) no analysis of ethical predicates and sentences in descriptive terms is possible.[9] The theory I am defending agrees with (a), is neutral about (b), and disagrees with (c).

Suppose, to fix the discussion, it turns out that rightness is maximizing expected hedonic value. What happens, that is, is that current folk morality evolves, or would evolve over time, into a mature folk morality that specifies a role for rightness that turns out, as a matter of fact, to be occupied by maximizing expected hedonic value.[10] Then, according to moral functionalism,

(3) Rightness = maximizing expected hedonic value.

So we agree that ethical properties are descriptive properties. But we were careful to refrain from committing ourselves to whether

(R) A is right iff $(\exists x_1) \ldots (A$ has x_r & $(y_1) \ldots (\mathbf{M}(y_1, \ldots))$ iff $x_1 = y_1$ & $\ldots))$

should be read as a piece of reference-fixing, or as a piece of meaning-giving, and so we remain neutral on the modal status of sentences like (3) that identify ethical properties with descriptive properties.

---

[9] See e.g. Richard Boyd, 'How to be a Moral Realist', in Geoffrey Sayre-McCord, ed., *Essays on Moral Realism* (Ithaca, NY: Cornell University Press, 1988), 181–228, and Peter Railton, 'Reply to David Wiggins', in John Haldane and Crispin Wright, eds., *Reality, Representation and Projection* (New York: Oxford University Press, 1993), 315–28. In Stephen Darwall, Allan Gibbard, and Peter Railton, 'Toward *Fin de Siècle* Ethics: Some Trends', *Philosophical Review*, 101 (1992): 115–89, views of the kind I have in mind here appear under two heads, as versions of post-positivistic nonreductive naturalism, see especially the remarks on p. 171, and as versions of reductive naturalism that appeal to synthetic identities, see esp. the remarks on p. 174.

[10] In saying that it is a matter of fact which property will turn out to occupy the rightness role in mature folk morality, I make a disputable assumption. It seems to me that there would be something deeply misguided about a moral system that allowed that everyone doing what they ought to do, what is right, made most of us very unhappy: a constraint on an acceptable mature folk morality is that it should end up with an account of what rightness is that does not have this consequence. But it is an empirical matter what makes people happy. Moreover, the output clauses of mature folk morality will concern the kinds of properties that motivate us to some degree, or in some idealized circumstances, or whatever, and which properties these are is an empirical matter. However, the ecumenical nature of moral functionalism means that it is not a thesis of moral functionalism *per se* that it is an empirical matter (in the sense of being a posteriori) which properties occupy which roles in mature folk morality. I am indebted here to Philip Pettit and Michael Smith.

Analytical Descriptivism

There is, however, a clear disagreement over the question of analysis. I am committed to the possibility of giving purely descriptive truth-conditions for ethical predications (as we noted earlier). Because the right-hand side of (R) does not contain any ethical terms, (R) as a whole constitutes an account of when *A* is right in purely descriptive terms, in contradiction to the anti-analysis, anti-reductionist theme in Cornell realism.

It is, of course, true that we are not putting (R) forward as an analysis of rightness according to *current* folk morality: (R) comes from mature folk morality. It is also true that we are remaining neutral on whether (R) is analytic in the sense of being a priori and necessary. This follows from our neutrality on the question of whether (R) is a piece of reference-fixing or a piece of meaning-giving. Nevertheless, we take the identification of rightness, and the moral properties in general, albeit those as identified in mature not current folk morality, to depend on offering an analysis in the sense of an a priori story about rightness that proceeds entirely in descriptive terms, and this is a clear disagreement with the Cornell position. We say, and the Cornell position denies, that, at the end of the day, we can say all there is to say about ethical nature in descriptive terms.

It is convenient to have a name for what is in common between positions that agree in espousing a descriptive metaphysics and ontology for ethical properties, while differing over the possibility of a descriptive analysis of ethical terms. I will, somewhat arbitrarily, use 'metaphysical descriptivism' for what we agree about, reserve 'ontological descriptivism' for the anti-analysis position occupied by the Cornell realists, and use 'analytical descriptivism' for our version of metaphysical descriptivism.[11]

The Case for an Analytical Style of Descriptivism

I think the commitment to the analytical style of metaphysical descriptivism is a strength rather than a weakness of our position. For it is common ground with the ontological descriptivists that there is no ethical nature over and above descriptive nature. If we

---

[11] Analytical descriptivism is opposed under the name of 'definitional naturalism' in Smith, *The Moral Problem*. In what follows I am much indebted to discussions with him (in which neither of us succeeded in convincing the other).

say enough about the descriptive way things are, we must include the ethical way things are. This follows from the metaphysical descriptivism concerning ethical nature that we and the Cornell realists agree about. But then we can tell the whole story in descriptive terms alone, and we should be able to sketch how to do this: if the distinctions we draw in ethical language do not outrun those we are able to draw in descriptive language, we should be able to sketch how to match up the distinctions we draw in the two vocabularies. This is precisely what we are offering for the term 'right' when we put forward (R). The fact that the right-hand side of (R) contains no ethical terminology means that (R) constitutes a story about how the descriptive story makes true that aspect of the ethical story particularly concerning rightness. This is what makes (R)—and its companions for the other ethical terms—our answer to the location problem for ethics. But if we follow the lead of ontological descriptivism and refuse to advance any kind of analysis, we are, it seems to me, ducking what is, in David Armstrong's term, a compulsory question for metaphysical descriptivists in ethics. We are refusing to come clean on what aspects of descriptive nature make true, or determine without remainder, accounts given in ethical terms.

I know from experience that many are unmoved by this argument. They insist that it is completely open to them to be good metaphysical descriptivists (and naturalists cum physicalists in the philosophy of mind sense, they often add) in ethics, while holding that there are no analyses of the ethical in terms of the descriptive to be had; there are no a priori connections that take us from descriptive accounts to ethical accounts of matters. So let me labour the point a little.

It is not a miracle that the word 'right' picks out the property it does pick out. It is a function of how the world is, of how we take things to be, and of conventions of word usage. Moreover, metaphysical descriptivists think that how the world is, how we take things to be, and conventions of word usage, can be exhaustively given in purely descriptive terms. In consequence, they are committed to something like

(4) If things are so-and-so, then 'right' picks out P,

where P is descriptive, and the 'so-and-so' is the descriptively given account of how it is that 'right' picks out P. What is more, there should be something like (4) that holds independently of how things actually are. Of course, (4) *itself* might depend on how things actually are, but that would be because 'If things are actually such and such, then (4), but if . . ., not (4)' is true, in which case

(5) If things are so-and-so and such-and-such, then 'right' picks out P

would be true independently of how things actually are. In sum, by including enough in the antecedents, we can be sure that there is a raft of conditionals of the form

If things are D_i, then 'right' picks out P_i,

where the D_i and the P_i are all descriptive, each member of which is true independently of how things actually are—that is to say, each is a priori. But now we have an a priori account of when something is right in descriptive terms: A is right iff D_1 & A has P_1, or D_2 & A has P_2, or . . .

Ontological descriptivists often make much of the existence of true property identities '$P = Q$', where 'P' and 'Q' cannot be analysed in terms of each other. But the obvious examples fall into two classes. One is typified by

(6) Blue = the colour of the sky,[12]

and this example does not address the making-true question because it is contingent. The distribution of things with the colour of the sky neither determines, nor is determined by, the distribution of blue things. Or suppose that

(7) Three metres = the height of the tallest man

is true. It is not an answer to what determines without remainder that someone is the tallest man is that he is three metres tall; what determines his being the tallest is his being taller than any other man.

The other example is typified by our old friend

(8) Water = H_2O.

---

[12] Some may not want to call this an identity statement because it contains a definite description, but what to call the sentence is not important for the points that follow.

In this case the corresponding determination claim is true. It is true, for instance, that the H_2O way things are makes true the water way things are. For example, the distribution of H_2O necessitates the distribution of water: nothing more needs to be true for there to be water in front of me than for there to be H_2O in front of me. But the connection between water and H_2O is a classic case of an a posteriori necessity. Hence, it might seem, we have an example of full determination by a property identity that is not answerable to analytical claims, and so one suitable as a model for the ontological descriptivist in ethics.

But we saw in Chapters 2 and 3 that this would be a mistake. True, the passage from

(9) H_2O covers most of the Earth

to

(10) Water covers most of the Earth

is not a conceptual entailment. But the passage from (9) conjoined with

(9a) H_2O is the watery stuff of our acquaintance

to (10) is a conceptual entailment. As we argued in the earlier chapters (and so I will make the point quickly here), a rich enough story about the H_2O way things are does conceptually entail the water way things are, and the way to see this is via the a priori truth that water is the watery stuff of our acquaintance.[13]

Ontological descriptivists have, of course, a serious motivation for denying the possibility of an analysis of the ethical in descriptive terms. They hold that analytical descriptivism is refuted by one or another version of the open question argument. What they like about their version of the view that ethical properties are identical with descriptive properties is that it allows that it makes perfect sense to question any and every thesis about how the ethical way things are is connected to the descriptive way things are.[14] They typically grant that supervenience tells us that some

---

[13] If I understand them aright, a similar point is being made by Terence Horgan and Mark Timmons, 'Troubles for New Wave Moral Semantics: The "Open Question Argument" Revived', *Philosophical Papers*, 21 (1992): 153–90, see esp. 162.

[14] See e.g. Railton, 'Reply to David Wiggins'.

connections between ethical and descriptive nature hold of necessity, but as, according to their view, each and every such connection is a posteriori, each and every connection can sensibly be doubted[15]—just as Moore taught us. However, analytical descriptivism, or at least the style of analytical descriptivism being defended here, can, it seems to me, mount a good reply to the open question argument. The remainder of this chapter is concerned with this question. I start by distinguishing two versions of the open question challenge to analytical descriptivism.

THE OPEN QUESTION ARGUMENT

The Moorean Version

We can distinguish the Moorean version of the open question argument from the Humean version of the open question argument.[16] The Moorean version is the version that raises the general issue known as the paradox of analysis, and is the version dominant in Moore—or so it seems to me.[17] It turns on the claim that no matter how much information of a purely descriptive kind I have, and no matter how carefully I have digested it and put it all together, it is still open to me to go either way on such questions as: Is *A* good? Is *A* what I ought to do? and, Is *A* right? Any and every identification of some descriptively given situation as good, or as what ought to be done, or as right, is itself a substantive ethical position. But then, runs the argument, how can the connection between the descriptively given way things are and the ethically given way things are be a priori?

But what exactly is supposed to be always and genuinely an open question? Any and every identification of rightness, say, with some descriptive property? But this claim could be no objection to moral functionalist styles of analytical descriptivism. The identifications of ethical properties with moral properties offered by moral functionalism are one and all a posteriori. What is a priori

---

[15] Or better, each and every *interesting* connection. We can all agree that something like 'if Jones does not exist then Jones has done no wrong' is a priori.

[16] For a similar distinction in different words, see Darwall, Gibbard, and Railton, 'Toward *Fin de Siècle* Ethics', 115–17.

[17] See e.g. Moore, *Principia Ethica*, ch. 1.

according to moral functionalism is not that rightness is such-and-such a descriptive property, but rather that *A* is right if and only if *A* has whatever property it is that plays the rightness role in mature folk morality, and it is an a posteriori matter what that property is.

True, according to moral functionalism, a sufficiently rich descriptive story leads a priori to an act's being right; but this will be a clear case of an unobvious a priori or conceptual entailment, precisely because of the complexity of the moral functionalist story. Just as we can sensibly doubt the result of a long, complex numerical addition by virtue of its making sense to doubt that the addition was done correctly (and, consequently, insist that a statement of the result of the addition is a 'substantive' position in arithmetic, and that it is 'open' to us to query the answer), so we can make sense of doubting the result of the complex story that moral functionalism says leads from the descriptive to the ethical. Moreover, what matters according to moral functionalism is the nature of *mature* folk morality; the shape of the theory current folk morality will (or would) turn into, or converge on, under critical reflection. For that is what settles the rightness role, and, thereby, when combined with the relevant facts about which properties occupy which roles, the property rightness is. Thus, there will, here and now, inevitably be a substantial degree of 'openness' induced by the very fact that the rightness role is currently under negotiation.

It may be objected that even when all the negotiation and critical reflection is over and we have arrived at mature folk morality, it will still make perfect sense to doubt that the right is what occupies the rightness role. But now I think that we analytical descriptivists are entitled to dig in our heels and insist that the idea that what fits the bill *that* well might still fail to be rightness, is nothing more than a hangover from the platonist conception that the meaning of a term like 'right' is somehow a matter of its picking out, or being mysteriously attached to, the form of the right.

It is worth noting here that non-cognitivists also have to say that something can seem to be a genuinely open question when it is really a closed one, though unobviously so. Non-cognitivists like to argue that if you think of a word like 'right' as expressing an attitude of a certain kind (one that stands up to a certain kind of scrutiny, perhaps), or as giving voice to a certain kind of recommendation (a rationally defensible one, say), or as serving to prescribe in a certain kind of way (the way that can be universalized, as it might be), there is a simple answer as to why saying '*A* is . . ., but *A* is not right', where the ellipsis is filled with something purely descriptive, always seems to be open to one: the word 'right' recommends rather than describes, and it is never inconsistent to refrain from recommending *A* no matter what description you give *A*. They argue that it seems open because it *is* open, and so they have no need to deny the appearances. However, matters are not that simple.

Recommendations (and prescriptions, etc., but I will make the point for recommendation versions of non-cognitivism) supervene on descriptive nature: two worlds exactly alike in descriptive nature are exactly alike in what is recommended, in what way, and by whom. Moreover, non-cognitivists typically insist that their view does not traffic in metaphysical mysteries: their recommendations can be exhaustively described in purely descriptive terms (and, they often add, as good naturalists in the philosophy of mind sense, in purely naturalistic cum physicalist terms). But now consider the status they must give sentences of the form 'I am recommending *A* in . . . a manner, but *A* is not right', where the ellipsis is filled with their favourite account of the special kind of recommendation that is moral recommendation. As deniers of metaphysical mysteries, they allow that we can give these favourite accounts in purely descriptive terms. But this means that, in their view, sentences like these amount to pragmatic contradictions: the first part of the sentence says that the speaker is making a recommendation of a certain kind, while the second part of the sentence actually *makes* the opposite recommendation. They are like 'I am commanding you to shut the door, but do not shut it'. Again, there will be, on their view, something of the form '*A* is right but I am not recommending it in . . . a manner', where the ellipsis is filled with something purely descriptive, which is a pragmatic contradiction: the first part makes a recommendation that the second part reports as not being made.

Now it is tempting to insist that no matter what spelling-out of the descriptive specification of the recommendations may be given, it is always perfectly sensible and non-pragmatically contradictory to say, '*A* is right, but I am not recommending it in . . . a manner', or to say, 'I am recommending *A* in . . . a manner, but *A* is not right'. But, of course, non-cognitivists must resist this temptation.

On their view, some such sentences *are* pragmatic contradictions. But this means that non-cognitivists, as well as cognitivists, must say that appearances can deceive, and, in consequence, must talk about unobvious, conceptual connections and the like. The only difference between us is over whether the (unobvious) contradictions in question should be described as pragmatic or not.

The Humean Version

The Humean version of the open question argument—the version, as it seems to me, that we find in R. M. Hare[18]—can be seen as bolstering the Moorean version. The bolstered version of the open question argument insists that the real point behind the argument is not *that* it always makes sense to ask what I ought to do no matter how much descriptive information I have, but *why* it always makes sense. To accept an ethical account of some situation is *per se* to take up an essentially directed attitude towards it, whereas accepting a descriptive account of it can never be *in itself* the taking up of a directed attitude towards it—thus the openness of questions like: Is *A* good? and, Is *A* right or what I ought to? in the face of complete descriptive information.

On the Humean construal, the real force of the open question argument is not met by the usual reminders about unobvious conceptual connections and the paradox of analysis; it can only be met by showing how belief about the way things are can have a direction built into it. The remainder of this chapter is devoted to explaining how beliefs about the way things are, and, in particular, about the ethical way things are on the purely descriptive account that moral functionalism offers of such beliefs, can have a direction built into them.

DESCRIPTIVISM AND THE DIRECTED NATURE OF MORAL JUDGEMENT

To judge that *A* is right is, according to cognitivism, to have a belief about how things are, including especially how *A* is. What is

---

[18] R. M. Hare, *The Language of Morals* (Oxford: Clarendon Press, 1952), see esp. § 5. 6.

more, according to moral functionalism, moral judgements are complex beliefs about the descriptive way things are. The hard question we have left to the end is that of explaining how such a belief can have the essentially directed nature distinctive of the judgement that *A* is right. A similar question arises of course for the judgement that *A* is wrong, except that this time the direction is away from *A*, and for ethical judgement in general, except that the sense in which the judgement is directed in other cases is more complex.

Two Cognitivist Strategies Distinguished

One cognitivist strategy is to hold that the judgement that *A* is right is simply a belief whose content is special in that having a belief with that content in and of itself points towards doing *A*. I will call this the content strategy. It is the strategy followed by John McDowell and Mark Platts, and, in an importantly different form, by Michael Smith.[19]

The second strategy agrees with the first that the judgement that *A* is right is a belief proper, and agrees that the content of the belief points towards doing *A*, but insists that there is more to be said, namely, that the typical way of *having* a belief with the content that *A* is right involves some kind of desire or motivation towards *A*. Philip Pettit and I call this strategy the content-possession strategy, because it adds to a view about the content of the belief that *A* is right, a view about what is typically involved in having or possessing a belief with that content. This is the strategy for answering the non-cognitivists' challenge I will be defending, but first we need to address the content strategy.

Two Anti-Humean and One Humean Version of the Content Strategy

The content strategy comes in a Humean, and two anti-Humean, forms. In one anti-Humean form, the view is that the content of

---

[19] John McDowell, 'Values and the Secondary Qualities', in Ted Honderich, ed., *Morality and Objectivity* (London: Routledge & Kegan Paul, 1985), 110–29; Mark Platts, 'Moral Reality and the End of Desire', in Mark Platts, ed., *Reference, Truth and Reality* (London: Routledge & Kegan Paul, 1981), 69–82; and Smith, *The Moral Problem*.

the belief that *A* is right is such that having a belief with such a content in and of itself can motivate one to some extent towards doing *A* in the absence of any desire or pro-attitude towards *A*. I think we should set this style of anti-Humean view aside. Hume did enough, it seems to me, to show that the very fact that a belief motivates to some extent *entails* facts about accompanying desires.[20] There need not be accompanying desires in the sense of *yearnings*, or anything like that, but the very fact of motivation to some extent by belief entails relevant facts about agents' pro-attitudes. The interesting anti-Humean version of the content strategy allows that there must be relevant pro-attitudes whenever belief motivates, but insists that in the case of beliefs like that *A* is right, the relevant pro-attitudes may be entailed by the belief itself, and in that sense are not a separate ingredient in the story. The idea is not that we can have motivation without both belief and desire, but that we can have motivation without *more* by way of desire than is entailed by belief alone.

The Humean version of the content strategy denies that believing that *A* is right entails anything about desires—first-order, second-order, hypothetical, or whatever. Its claim is that the content of what is believed when we believe that something is right in itself points towards *A* by virtue of being a belief in part about desires—first-order, second-order, hypothetical, or whatever. On this account, to judge something right is to believe *inter alia* something about what is desired, is desired to be desired, would be desired in ideal circumstances, or whatever, of a kind that points towards *A*.

Moral Functionalism and the Content Strategy

Moral functionalists who want to follow the content strategy must, I think, follow the Humean version. For they would have to hold a particularly controversial version of the anti-Humean doctrine that the belief that *A* is right entails something about the holder's desire for *A*. For moral functionalists hold that the belief that *A* is right is a purely descriptive one; it is the belief that *A* has whatever (descriptive) property stands in certain purely descriptively specifiable relations to various other descriptive properties. They would, therefore, have to hold that having a belief with a

[20] *Pace*, as I understand him, Platts, 'Moral Reality and the End of Desire'.

purely descriptive content entails facts about what one desires. This is hard to believe.[21]

Moreover, moral functionalism lends itself to a simple implementation of the Humean version of the content strategy. Moral functionalism sees the meanings of the moral terms as given by their place in a network. Part of that network are certain output clauses that tell us how beliefs about ethical properties connect with facts about motivation. The details of these output clauses are highly controversial. But, to fix the discussion, let's suppose that the connection with motivation goes roughly as follows—and here I choose a formulation partly because it is of a kind that is widely entertained in one form or another, and partly because it seems to me to be on essentially the right lines[22]—right act is one that has properties of value to an extent that exceeds that of the various alternatives to it, and a property's value depends on its being rational for us to desire it. The *moral* rightness of action is, then, a matter of its having properties of value which are the kind of properties that pertain to morality rather than, say, prudence— where the demarcation of the moral from the prudential will itself be part of mature folk morality.

It is important to this sort of proposal that we can give an account of what makes it *rational* to desire a property that does not reduce, uselessly, to its being a rightness-making property. Perhaps

---

[21]   More precisely, what is hard to believe is that the belief that *A* is right *per se*, on moral functionalists' account of that belief, entails having any particular desires. It may be that there are certain desires entailed by the very fact of having any beliefs at all. David Lewis, 'Desire as Belief II', *Mind*, 105 (1996): 303–13, points out that you might well argue that there are certain desires that anyone who has any states properly described as beliefs must have. It is widely accepted that anyone who has states that count as beliefs must have some desires or other—this follows from the way belief and desire are interdefined—the possible position insists in addition that there are some desires that must be had if any states are to count as beliefs.

[22]   An account of somewhat the kind that follows is to be found in Smith, *The Moral Problem*. I should note, in order to avoid possible confusion, that Smith there calls a view anti-Humean, if it violates a Humean thesis about *rationality*, namely, that a course of action is rational only to the extent that it serves an agents' desires given their beliefs, and that belief alone never determines whether or not a course of action is rational. He is especially concerned to argue that this view of Hume's on rationality is mistaken. We are calling a view anti-Humean if it violates a connected but distinct Humean thesis about *cognitive states*, namely, that *what* you believe *per se* never entails facts about desires.

the properties it is rational to desire are the ones we would desire to desire after critical reflection on, and full acquaintance with, them; perhaps they are the properties our idealized selves, possibly in the guise of the ideal observer, would desire, or would desire to desire; perhaps they are the properties our idealized selves would converge on desiring after discussion; perhaps they are the most stable of our long-term desires; perhaps they are the desires we are prepared to universalize in the sense of being the desires we would allow anyone and everyone to act on; . . . The details will not matter for what follows. What will matter, though, is something I take to be widely agreed, perhaps under the heading of the rejection of platonism about value, perhaps under the heading of the response-dependence of value. It is that what confers value on a property ultimately comes down to facts about desires: value supervenes on the total story, actual, hypothetical, first- and higher-order, or something of this general kind, about desire. Accordingly, this much is right in subjectivism about value: what gives value whatever objectivity it has comes down, somehow or other, to some combination of facts about the convergence, the stability, the coherence between first-order and higher-order desires, the desires of idealizations of ourselves, the desires of our community, and the like.

Moral functionalism's implementation of the Humean version of the content strategy is now easy to give. To believe that A is right is to believe that A has the property that fills the rightness role, and part of this role is to be the property (or one of the properties, but allowing ourselves disjunctive properties means that we can talk of *the* property) that it is rational for us to desire. Thus, to believe that A is right is *inter alia* to believe that A has the property it is rational to desire. And this surely is to have a belief that points towards doing A. We moral functionalists can, thus, explain the directed nature of the belief that A is right, within a purely descriptive framework and without buying into an argument with Hume on the distinctness of belief and desire.

The Content-Possession Strategy: Adding Motivation to Direction

We now have a story about what is believed when it is believed that A is right that can be regarded as pointing towards A. When you believe that *A* is right, you believe in part that *A* has properties it is rational to desire all things considered.[23]

It would, though, be good to find something more for the cognitivist to say. The relevant facts about your desire profile—and the desire profiles of your community if they are included as part of the story—that make it rational to desire *A* can obtain in the absence of even a whiff of current motivation towards *A*. They are essentially facts about hypothetical, idealized, possibly second-order, desires, and the like; they are not about what you want here and now, not even about what you want here and now defeasibly. This is true on any of the extant proposals for analysing what makes a desire rational. We are, therefore, short of an explanation as to why *typically* belief that *A* is right goes along with at least some degree of motivation towards *A*. The content story tells us how the belief that *A* is right points towards *A* in the sense of involving a belief about hypothetical desires, or some such, that point towards *A*, but it does not explain how typically, though not invariably, the very *holding* of the belief that *A* is right goes along with some kind of current motivation in favour of *A*, or at least some sort of leaning towards *A* that, as it is sometimes put, *colours* the way *A* presents itself to one who believes that it is the right thing to do. Moreover, the belief that you and your kind would in ideal circumstances desire to do *A*—I assume this account of rationality of desire for the purpose of making the point—may be quite false. We are far from infallible about what we would desire—as anyone who has gone to a football match expecting to barrack for one team but finds themselves barracking for the opposition, well knows.

There is, I think, 'something more' that the cognitivist can say. It appeals to the content-possession strategy (to use Philip Pettit's term, though he should not be held responsible for my way of putting the idea).

It is a familiar idea that to be red is, roughly, to be such as to look red to normal persons in normal circumstances—though, as we noted in Chapter 4, this does not mean that red should be identified with the disposition to look red in normal circumstances. It follows that to believe that *A* is red is to believe that *A* is such that

---

[23] See Smith, *The Moral Problem*, though he presents it as a theory opposed to moral functionalism, I am sorry to say.

it looks red to normal persons in normal circumstances. But most of us are not experts on the characterization of normal circumstances, on the relation between being red and looking red, and the role of the opinions of others in determining when one's own colour judgements are mistaken: to become such an expert involves addressing the issues that concern philosophers of colour, and most of us who believe that something is red are not philosophers of colour. We count as believing that something is some colour or other, not by virtue of our ability to affirm certain complex sentences concerning colour, but by virtue of dispositions to form colour judgements in the appropriate circumstances—that is how we manifest our acceptance of the relevant notion of normal conditions, and the importance of the opinions of others about colour for how justified our colour judgements are. Likewise, it is possible to accept *modus ponens* without being a logician—that is, without being able to write down the relevant logical rule in some formal system. In most people, what constitutes their acceptance of *modus ponens* is their readiness to infer in accord with it.

Now, on the moral functionalist story, to believe that something is right is to believe in part that it is what we would in ideal circumstances desire, where we can regard the rubric 'would in ideal circumstances desire' as covering the possible spellings-out already mentioned—perhaps what we would desire in ideal circumstances is what we would desire when our first-order desires square with our reflective second-order desires, or when our desires square with what we would converge on stably desiring after reflection, perhaps taking into account the desires of our community, or something along these gestured-at lines. And what shows this is of a kind with what shows the content of the belief that something is red, namely, the circumstances in which we form the belief in question. The fact that a belief that something is red is in part a belief about normal circumstances is shown by the situations in which we form the belief that something is red. Likewise, what shows that the belief that A is right is in part a belief about what would be ideally desired, is that we form it when it is true that we would in ideal circumstances desire A.

Now this fact will typically manifest itself in our feeling to some degree the 'tug' of A. Think of a situation when you do not desire a cold beer but know that you will later in the day. Perhaps you are about to mow the lawn on a hot day. You have beforehand no inclination towards beer-drinking: you aren't thirsty, and it is too early in the day for alcohol to be attractive. But you know that after mowing the lawn you will desire a cold beer, and will enjoy drinking one. Even before you have any desire for beer, your awareness that you will later desire beer places the idea of beer in an attractive light, indeed one that helps motivate you to mow the lawn. I think the same is true of the belief that A is right. We form the belief that A is right when we are disposed to desire it in ideal circumstances, and this very fact typically colours our way of thinking of A in a way that makes it attractive, that explains the prick of conscience, our sense of unease, when we fail to do what we judge we ought to do. This does not have to be the case, of course. Expert psychologists might assure you, and you might believe them, that despite A's not exerting the slightest pull on you at the moment, and your not being aware that it would, nevertheless in more ideal circumstances it would. You would then take a kind of 'third person' view of yourself; you believe all sorts of things about what you would desire in ideal circumstances, on the basis of what others tell you rather than on the basis of how things present themselves to you. But these cases are the exception. Normally, we know 'from the inside' that A would be desired in ideal circumstances, and when we do, A acquires the 'coloration' we associate with judging that something is right, and which can, when all goes well, motivate us towards doing it.

The content-possession strategy adds this point about coloration to the directional story the content strategy tells in order to account for the motivational element typically associated with believing that A is right.

Postscript

When I have presented this material in the past, I have met two protests from non-cognitivists. The first protest insists that when one judges, *really* judges, that A is right, one must have a current, first-order pro-attitude towards A: beliefs about what one would desire, or about desires to desire, and all the rest of it, are, it is urged, not enough. I don't myself take this view, but I can see how one might and I think it is an advantage of moral functionalism that it can take it on board. Moral functionalists can view moral judgement as a species of belief in part defined by being accompanied by the relevant pro-attitude. In our terms, what the protesters are insisting is that it is part of current folk morality—and so central a part that it must be retained in any mature folk morality—that a moral judgement is accompanied by the relevant pro-attitude (or con-attitude if the judgement is that something is wrong, say). And we can accommodate this view by refusing to *call* something a *moral* belief unless it is accompanied by the relevant pro-attitude. The protesters sometimes insist that this reply is a 'cheat'. But how can it be a cheat if I am giving them exactly what they insist on?

The second non-cognitivist protest points out that, on the story I have told, if X and Y agree about *all* the descriptive facts and are not confused in their thinking, then they cannot disagree, in the sense of coming to judgements with different truth-values, about the ethical facts. For, on the story I have told, ethical judgements are highly complex descriptive judgements. But surely, runs the protest, despite full and unconfused agreement about the descriptively given facts, X might say 'A is right', and Y say 'A is not right' without it *following* that they must mean something at least slightly different by the word 'right': genuine moral disagreement is possible between two people even if they agree about all the descriptive facts and are not confused.

My reply to this objection comes in two parts. First, I think that some of its appeal is a hangover from platonism about value; the idea that somehow terms like 'right' and 'good' latch onto non-natural features of reality independently of the descriptive situations in which we use the terms. Once we turn our backs on platonism and Moore, I think we have to face the fact that what we mean by these terms is somehow or other a matter of the situations descriptively given—including, of course, the relevant facts about actual, possible, and higher-order desires—in which we use them. And so, if two people agree on the descriptively given facts, are not confused, and one uses 'right' to describe a given situation and the other does not, they mean something different by the terms—or at least they do on one reasonable meaning of 'meaning'.

Secondly, it is hard to see how we have here a point in favour of non-cognitivism. I and non-cognitivists like Blackburn and Gibbard agree that we can 'tell it all' in descriptive terms. The distinctive feature of non-cognitivism is the claim that a sentence like

'*A* is right' expresses rather than reports a certain sort of attitude; this is how producing the sentence counts as recommending (or prescribing, etc.) rather than asserting. And, of course, if the sentence reported the attitude, we would have a version of *cognitivism*—one which held that '*A* is right' is true in a person's mouth just if they have the attitude reported. Now, how precisely is this view supposed to preserve the possibility of genuine moral disagreement in the face of complete and unconfused agreement between *X* and *Y* on the descriptive facts—that is, all the facts? The only possible answer, and the one given by non-cognitivists, is by virtue of the fact that *X* and *Y* might have different attitudes to, say, *A*. But if that counts as disagreement, what are we buying with the non-cognitivism? Consider cognitivists who hold that '*A* is right' reports the attitude instead of, as the non-cognitivists hold, expressing it. They can equally have moral disagreement in the face of complete agreement about the descriptive facts *in the proffered sense*. If a certain difference in attitudes counts as a genuine disagreement, it does so quite independently of whether it is best to hold that certain *sentences* express such attitudes or to hold that they report them.

BIBLIOGRAPHY

Adams, Ernest. *The Logic of Conditionals*. Dordrecht: Reidel, 1975.

Adams, Fred and Stecker, Robert. 'Vacuous Singular Terms', *Mind and Language*, 9 (1994): 387–401.

Armstrong, D. M. *A Combinatorial Theory of Possibility*. Cambridge: Cambridge University Press, 1989.

—— *A Materialist Theory of the Mind*. London: Routledge & Kegan Paul, 1968.

—— 'Identity through Time', in P. van Inwagen, ed., *Time and Cause: Essays Presented to Richard Taylor*. Dordrecht: Reidel, 1980, pp. 67–78.

—— *Universals and Scientific Realism*, 2 vols. Cambridge: Cambridge University Press, 1978.

Ayer, A. J. *Language, Truth and Logic*. London: Victor Gollancz, 1962.

—— 'On the Analysis of Moral Judgements', repr. in *Philosophical Essays*. London: Macmillan, 1959, pp. 231–49.

—— *The Problem of Knowledge*. London: Macmillan, 1956.

Bennett, Jonathan. 'Substance, Reality, and Primary Qualities', repr. in C. B. Martin and D. M. Armstrong, eds., *Locke and Berkeley*. New York: Doubleday, 1968.

Bigelow, John and Pargetter, Robert. *Science and Necessity*. Cambridge: Cambridge University Press, 1990.

Blackburn, Simon. 'Supervenience Revisited', in Ian Hacking, ed., *Exercises in Analysis: Essays by Students of Casimir Lewy*. Cambridge: Cambridge University Press, 1985.

Block, Ned. 'Can the Mind Change the World?', in G. Boolos, ed., *Meaning and Method: Essays in Honor of Hilary Putnam*. Cambridge: Cambridge University Press, 1990.

—— 'Psychologism and Behaviorism', *Philosophical Review*, 90 (1981): 5–43.

Boghossian, Paul. 'The Status of Content', *Philosophical Review*, 99 (1990): 157–84.

Boyd, Richard. 'How to be a Moral Realist', in Geoffrey Sayre-McCord, ed., *Essays on Moral Realism*. Ithaca, NY: Cornell University Press, 1988, pp. 181–228.

Campbell, John. 'A Simple View of Colour', in John Haldane and Crispin Wright, eds., *Reality, Representation, and Projection*. New York: Oxford University Press, 1993, pp. 257–68.

Campbell, John (I. G.) and Pargetter, Robert. 'Goodness and Fragility', *American Philosophical Quarterly*, 23 (1986): 155–66.

Campbell, Keith. 'Colours', in Robert Brown and C. D. Rollins, eds., *Contemporary Philosophy in Australia*. London: Allen & Unwin, 1969, pp. 132–57.

Carroll, Lewis. *Through the Looking Glass and What Alice Saw There*, in *The Annotated Alice*, ed. Martin Gardner. Harmondsworth: Penguin, 1965.

Castañeda, Hector-Neri. 'He*: A Study in the Logic of Self-Consciousness', *Ratio*, 8 (1966): 130–57.

Chalmers, David. *The Conscious Mind*. New York: Oxford University Press, 1996.

Charles, David. 'Supervenience, Composition, and Physicalism', in David Charles and Kathleen Lennon, eds., *Reduction, Explanation, and Realism*. Oxford: Clarendon Press, 1992, pp. 265–96.

Child, William. 'Anomalism, Uncodifiability, and Psychophysical Relations', *Philosophical Review*, 102 (1993): 215–45.

Chisholm, Roderick M. *Perceiving*. Ithaca, NY: Cornell University Press, 1957.

Churchland, Patricia. *Neurophilosophy*. Cambridge, Mass.: MIT Press, 1986.

Churchland, Paul. 'Eliminative Materialism and the Propositional Attitudes', *Journal of Philosophy*, 78 (1981): 67–90.

—— 'Folk Psychology and the Explanation of Human Behaviour', *Proceedings of the Aristotelian Society*, supp. vol. 62 (1988): 209–21.

Crane, Tim and Mellor, D. H. ' There is No Question of Physicalism', *Mind*, 99 (1990): 185–206.

Darwall, Stephen, Gibbard, Allan, and Railton, Peter. 'Toward *Fin de Siècle* Ethics: Some Trends', *Philosophical Review*, 101 (1992): 115–89.

Davidson, Donald. 'Thinking Causes', in John Heil and Al Mele, eds., *Mental Causation*. Oxford: Clarendon Press, 1993, pp. 3–17.

Davies, Martin and Humberstone, I. L. 'Two Notions of Necessity', *Philosophical Studies*, 38 (1980): 1–30.

Dennett, Daniel C. *Consciousness Explained*. Boston, Mass.: Little Brown & Co., 1991.

Dummett, Michael. *Frege: Philosophy of Language*. London: Duckworth, 1973.

Edgington, Dorothy. 'Do Conditionals have Truth Conditions?', in Frank Jackson, ed., *Conditionals*. Oxford: Oxford University Press, 1991, pp. 176–201.

Evans, Gareth. *Collected Papers*. Oxford: Clarendon Press, 1985.

—— 'Reference and Contingency', *Monist*, 62 (1979): 161–89.

—— *The Varieties of Reference*. Oxford: Clarendon Press, 1982.

Field, Hartry. *Science without Numbers*. Oxford: Basil Blackwell, 1980.

Forrest, Peter. 'Universals and Universalisability', *Australasian Journal of Philosophy*, 70 (1992): 93–8.

—— 'Ways Worlds Could Be', *Australasian Journal of Philosophy*, 64 (1986): 15–24.

Geach, P. T. 'Some Problems about Time', in *Logic Matters*. Oxford: Basil Blackwell, 1972, pp. 302–18.

Gettier, Edmund. 'Is Justified True Belief Knowledge?', *Analysis*, 23 (1963): 121–3.

Gibbard, Allan. *Wise Choices: Apt Feelings*. Cambridge, Mass.: Harvard University Press, 1990.

Glover, Jonathan. *Causing Death and Saving Lives*. Harmondsworth: Penguin, 1977.

Grayling, A. C. *An Introduction to Philosophical Logic*. Brighton: Harvester Press, 1982.

Hardin, C. L. 'Are "Scientific" Objects Coloured?', *Mind*, 93 (1984): 491–500.

Hare, R. M. *Freedom and Reason*. Oxford: Clarendon Press, 1963.

—— *The Language of Morals*. Oxford: Clarendon Press, 1952.

Harman, Gilbert. 'Doubts about Conceptual Analysis', in John O'Leary Hawthorne and Michaelis Michael, eds., *Philosophy in Mind*. Dordrecht: Kluwer, 1994, pp. 43–8.

Harman, Gilbert. *The Nature of Morality*. New York: Oxford University Press, 1977.

Heal, Jane. *Fact and Meaning: Quine and Wittgenstein on Philosophy of Language*. Oxford: Basil Blackwell, 1989.

Hilbert, David R. *Color and Color Perception: A Study in Anthropocentric Realism*. Stanford, Calif.: CSLI, 1987.

Hilbert, David R. 'What is Color Vision?', *Philosophical Studies*, 68 (1992): 351–70.

Horgan, Terence. 'From Supervenience to Superdupervenience: Meeting the Demands of a Material World', *Mind*, 102 (1993): 555–86.

—— 'Supervenience and Microphysics', *Pacific Philosophical Quarterly*, 63 (1982): 29–43.

—— and Timmons, Mark. 'Troubles for New Wave Moral Semantics: The "Open Question Argument" Revived', *Philosophical Papers*, 21 (1992): 153–90.

Horwich, Paul. 'Gibbard's Theory of Norms', *Philosophy and Public Affairs*, 22 (1993): 67–78.

Hurley, Susan. *Natural Reasons: Personality and Polity*. New York: Oxford University Press, 1989.

Jackson, Frank. 'A Note on Physicalism and Heat', *Australasian Journal of Philosophy*, 56 (1980): 26–34.

Jackson, Frank. 'Armchair Metaphysics', in John O'Leary Hawthorne and Michaelis Michael, eds., *Philosophy in Mind*. Dordrecht: Kluwer, 1994.

—— *Conditionals*. Oxford: Basil Blackwell, 1987.

—— Critical Notice of Susan Hurley, *Natural Reasons*, *Australasian Journal of Philosophy*, 70 (1992): 475–88.

—— 'Decision-Theoretic Consequentialism and the Nearest and Dearest Objection', *Ethics*, 101 (1991): 461–82.

—— 'Essentialism, Mental Properties and Causation', *Proceedings of the Aristotelian Society*, 95 (1995): 253–68.

—— 'Finding the Mind in the Natural World', in Roberto Casati, Barry Smith, and Graham White, eds., *Philosophy and the Cognitive Sciences: Proceedings of the 16th International Wittgenstein Symposium*. Vienna: Hölder–Pichler–Tempsky, 1994, pp. 101–12.

—— 'Metaphysics by Possible Cases', *Monist*, 77 (1994): 93–110.

—— 'Postscript', in Paul K. Moser and J. D. Trout, eds., *Contemporary Materialism*. London: Routledge, 1995, pp. 184–9.

—— 'The Primary Quality View of Color', in James Tomberlin, ed., *Philosophical Perspectives*, vol. x. Cambridge, Mass.: Basil Blackwell, 1996, pp. 199–219.

—— 'What Mary Didn't Know', *Journal of Philosophy*, 83 (1986): 291–5.

—— and Pargetter, Robert. 'An Objectivist's Guide to Subjectivism about Colour', *Revue International de Philosophie*, 41 (1987): 127–41.

—— and Pettit, Philip. 'Functionalism and Broad Content', *Mind*, 97 (1988): 381–400.

—— —— 'Moral Functionalism and Moral Motivation', *Philosophical Quarterly*, 45 (1995): 20–40.

Jeffrey, Richard. *The Logic of Decision*, 2nd edn. Chicago, Ill.: Chicago University Press, 1983.

Johnston, Mark. 'Dispositional Theories of Value', *Proceedings of the Aristotelian Society*, supp. vol. 63 (1989): 139–74.

—— 'How to Speak of the Colors', *Philosophical Studies*, 68 (1992): 221–63.

Kagan, Shelly. *The Limits of Morality*. Oxford: Clarendon Press, 1989.

Kaplan, David. 'Demonstratives', in Joseph Almog, John Perry, and Howard Wettstein, eds., *Themes from Kaplan*. New York: Oxford University Press, 1989, pp. 481–564.

Kim, Jaegwon. '"Strong" and "Global" Supervenience Revisited', in *Supervenience and Mind*. Cambridge: Cambridge University Press, 1993, pp. 79–108.

Kirk, Robert. 'From Physical Explicability to Full Blooded Materialism', *Philosophical Quarterly*, 29 (1979): 229–37.

Kripke, Saul. *Naming and Necessity*. Oxford: Basil Blackwell, 1980.

Kroon, Fred. 'Causal Descriptivism', *Australasian Journal of Philosophy*, 65 (1987): 1–17.

Lakoff, George. *Women, Fire, and Dangerous Things*. Chicago, Ill.: University of Chicago Press, 1987.

Lewis, David. 'An Argument for the Identity Theory', *Journal of Philosophy*, 63 (1966): 17–25.

—— 'Attitudes *De Dicto* and *De Se*,' *Philosophical Review*, 88 (1979): 513–43.

—— *Convention*. Cambridge, Mass.: Harvard University Press, 1969.

—— 'Desire as Belief II', *Mind*, 105 (1996): 303–13.

—— 'Dispositional Theories of Value', *Proceedings of the Aristotelian Society*, supp. vol. 63 (1989): 113–37.

—— 'Finkish Dispositions', *Philosophical Quarterly*, 47 (1997): 143–58.

—— 'General Semantics', repr. in *Philosophical Papers*, vol. i. New York: Oxford University Press, 1983.

—— 'How to Define Theoretical Terms', *Journal of Philosophy*, 67 (1970): 427–46.

—— 'Index, Context and Content', in Stig Kanger and Sven Öhman, eds., *Philosophy and Grammar*. Dordrecht: Reidel, 1981, pp. 79–100.

—— 'New Work for a Theory of Universals', *Australasian Journal of Philosophy*, 61 (1983): 343–77.

—— *On the Plurality of Worlds*. Oxford: Basil Blackwell, 1986.

—— 'Probabilities of Conditionals and Conditional Probabilities', *Philosophical Review*, 85 (1976): 297–315.

—— 'Psychophysical and Theoretical Identifications', *Australasian Journal of Philosophy*, 50 (1972): 249–58.

—— 'Reduction of Mind', in Samuel Guttenplan, ed., *A Companion to the Philosophy of Mind*. Oxford: Basil Blackwell, 1994, pp. 412–31.

Locke, John. *An Essay concerning Human Understanding*. Oxford: Clarendon Press, 1975.

Lockwood, Michael. *Mind, Brain and the Quantum*. Oxford: Basil Blackwell, 1989.

Lycan, William G. *Consciousness*. Cambridge, Mass.: MIT Press, 1987.

—— *Judgement and Justification*. Cambridge: Cambridge University Press, 1988.

Mackie, J. L. *Ethics: Inventing Right and Wrong*. Harmondsworth: Penguin, 1977.

—— *Problems from Locke*. Oxford: Clarendon Press, 1976.

Martin, C. B. 'Dispositions and Conditionals', *Philosophical Quarterly*, 44 (1994): 1–8.

McDowell, John. 'Values and the Secondary Qualities', in Ted Honderich, ed., *Morality and Objectivity*. London: Routledge & Kegan Paul, 1985, pp. 110–29.

Moore, G. E. 'A Reply to My Critics', in P. A. Schilpp, ed., *The Philosophy of G. E. Moore*. Chicago, Ill.: Northwestern University Press, 1942, pp. 533–677.

—— *Principia Ethica*. Cambridge: Cambridge University Press, 1929.

Nagel, Thomas. *The View from Nowhere*. New York: Oxford University Press, 1986.

—— 'What is it Like to be a Bat?', *Philosophical Review*, 83 (1974): 435–50.

Papineau, David. *Philosophical Naturalism*. Oxford: Basil Blackwell, 1993.

Peacocke, Christopher. *A Study of Concepts*. Cambridge, Mass.: MIT Press, 1992.

Perry, John. 'The Problem of the Essential Indexical', *Nous*, 13 (1979): 3–21.

Pettit, Philip. 'A Definition of Physicalism', *Analysis*, 53 (1993): 213–23.

—— 'Microphysicalism without Contingent Micro-Macro Laws', *Analysis*, 54 (1994): 253–7.

Platts, Mark. 'Moral Reality and the End of Desire', in Mark Platts, ed., *Reference, Truth and Reality*. London: Routledge & Kegan Paul, 1980, pp. 69–82.

Putnam, Hilary. 'Is Water Necessarily H_2O?' in James Conant, ed., *Realism with a Human Face*. Cambridge, Mass.: Harvard University Press, 1990, pp. 54–79.

—— 'It Ain't Necessarily So', *Journal of Philosophy*, 59 (1962): 658–71.

—— 'Pragmatism', *Proceedings of the Aristotelian Society*, 95 (1995): 291–306.

—— 'The Meaning of "Meaning"', in *Language, Mind and Reality*. Cambridge: Cambridge University Press, 1975.

Quine, W. V. 'Propositional Objects', in *Ontological Relativity and Other Essays*. New York: Columbia University Press, 1969, pp. 139–60.

—— 'Two Dogmas of Empiricism', repr. in *From a Logical Point of View*. New York: Harper & Row, 1963, pp. 20–46.

—— *Word and Object*. Cambridge, Mass.: MIT Press, 1960.

Railton, Peter. 'Reply to David Wiggins', in John Haldane and Crispin Wright, eds., *Reality, Representation and Projection*. New York: Oxford University Press, 1993, pp. 315–28.

Rawls, John. *A Theory of Justice*. Oxford: Oxford University Press, 1973.

Robinson, Denis. 'Matter, Motion and Humean Supervenience', *Australasian Journal of Philosophy*, 67 (1989): 394–409.

Searle, John. *The Rediscovery of the Mind*. Cambridge, Mass.: MIT Press, 1992.

Shoemaker, Sydney. 'Causality and Properties', in *Identity, Cause, and Mind*. Cambridge: Cambridge University Press, 1984, pp. 206–33.

—— *Identity, Cause, and Mind*. Cambridge: Cambridge University Press, 1984.

—— 'Identity, Properties, and Causality', in *Identity, Cause, and Mind*. Cambridge: Cambridge University Press, 1984, pp. 234–60.

Slote, Michael. 'The Theory of Important Criteria', *Journal of Philosophy*, 63 (1966): 211–24.

Smart, J. J. C. *Our Place in the Universe*. Oxford: Basil Blackwell, 1989.

—— 'Sensations and Brain Processes', *Philosophical Review*, 68 (1959): 141–56.

Smith, Michael. 'Colour, Transparency, Mind-Independence', in John Haldane and Crispin Wright, eds., *Reality, Representation, and Projection*. New York: Oxford University Press, 1993, pp. 269–77.

—— *The Moral Problem*. Oxford: Basil Blackwell, 1994.

Soames, Scott. Review of Gareth Evans, *Collected Papers*, *Journal of Philosophy*, 86 (1989): 141–56.

Sober, Elliott. 'Why Logically Equivalent Predicates May Pick Out Different Properties', *American Philosophical Quarterly*, 19 (1982): 183–90.

Stalnaker, Robert. 'Assertion', in P. Cole, ed., *Syntax and Semantics*, vol. ix. New York: Academic Press, 1978, pp. 315–32.

—— *Inquiry*. Cambridge, Mass.: MIT Press, 1984.

—— 'Possible Worlds', *Nous*, 10 (1976): 65–75.

Stich, Stephen. 'What is a Theory of Mental Representation?', *Mind*, 101 (1992): 243–61.

Strawson, Galen. '"Red" and Red', *Synthese*, 78 (1989): 193–232.

Taylor, Barry. 'Dummett's McTaggart', in Richard Heck, ed., *Logic, Language, and Reality: Essays in Honour Of Michael Dummett*. Oxford: Clarendon Press, forthcoming.

Tichy, Pavel. 'Kripke on Necessity A Posteriori', *Philosophical Studies*, 43 (1983): 225–41.

Tye, Michael. 'Naturalism and the Mental', *Mind*, 101 (1992): 421–41.

Van Inwagen, Peter. *An Essay on Free Will*. Oxford: Clarendon Press, 1983.

Vlach, Frank. '"Now" and "Then": A Formal Study in the Logic of Tense and Anaphora'. Ph.D. dissertation, University of California at Los Angeles, 1973.

Wettstein, Howard. 'Cognitive Significance without Cognitive Content', in Joseph Almog, John Perry, and Howard Wettstein, eds., *Themes from Kaplan*. New York: Oxford University Press, 1989, pp. 421–54.

Williams, Bernard. *Ethics and the Limits of Philosophy*. London: Fontana, 1985.

—— 'The Self and the Future', *Philosophical Review*, 79 (1970): 161–80.

Wright, Crispin. *Truth and Objectivity*. Cambridge, Mass.: Harvard University Press, 1992.

Yablo, Stephen. 'Mental Causation', *Philosophical Review*, 101 (1992): 245–80.

INDEX

Index